The Jesus Kids

The Jesus Kids

ROGER C. PALMS

Judson Press, Valley Forge

THE JESUS KIDS

International Standard Book No. 0-8170-0546-3
Library of Congress Catalog Card No. 72-166486

Printed in the U.S.A.

Contents

Preface

What's going on in the streets?

Newspapers and magazines have been quick to report the "Jesus Movement." Some have written it off as a fad; others have called it a spiritual revival.

As in any nationwide event, there are many sides and facets to the Jesus movement. To take one part and assume it is the whole is to be very badly misinformed.

The Jesus Kids is a comprehensive look at the events, attitudes, and problems of the Jesus movement.

This book was written in the streets. The author traveled to various parts of the United States, visiting communes, coffee houses, teen centers, and churches. He talked to the leaders of the Jesus kids, pastors, and even the police. But most of the time he walked the streets. Night and day he talked to the Jesus kids, listening, watching, probing, and sensing the movement.

The Jesus Kids is written to help people understand what is happening, why it is happening, and where the Christian church fits in. The author is a journalist, but he is first a pastor. As a journalist, he attempts to give an accurate report of the Jesus movement; as a pastor, he tells what the Jesus kids feel about themselves and the church.

The Jesus kids are not just street people, although the movement started on the streets. The thinking of the Jesus kids is everywhere, because the street culture that produced them is everywhere.

Ready or not, the church will have to pay attention to the Jesus kids.

1

The Gospel Blitz

"Jesus loves you!"

"Jesus is coming soon!"

"Do you know Jesus?"

In a cabin called Shepherd by the Sea in Ventura, California, five Christian beach boys witness to surfers about Jesus.

"Sometimes we pick them up hitchhiking," one of them explains. "Other times we meet them on the beach. Over the last couple of years, three thousand guys have come through the cabin."

Some only stay for a shower and a meal; others stay for several weeks. But everyone who comes to the cabin is told about Jesus, and many have accepted him as their personal Savior.

Near the lighted dome of Michigan's State Capitol in Lansing, high school and college young people move out of the Master's House to witness about Jesus to the scores of bored young people parked in their cars along Washington Avenue.

"See those kids?" Don asks, pointing. "We just walk from car to car telling them about Jesus Christ. If they get angry with us, we ask them what they've got against Jesus."

For Don and the other Jesus kids, witnessing for Jesus is what life is all about.

In California's Redondo Beach, former acid heads and dropouts are baptized in the Pacific surf. When they come out to the cheering crowds, they rejoice by hugging the first person they see. It's a new family, and all of the kids are their brothers and sisters.

From Sunset Strip in Hollywood to Seventeenth Street in

Nashville; Telegraph Avenue in Berkeley to Grand River Avenue in Detroit; Capitol Hill in Denver to Times Square in New York; Yale Park in Albuquerque to the quiet streets of Tecumseh, Michigan, the Jesus kids are spreading the message of salvation. With tracts and Bibles, they are taking to the streets in ever-increasing numbers, bearing witness to everyone they meet about the saving power of Jesus Christ.

Whether they are called "Jesus Freaks," "Jesus People," or "The Children of God," these ex-pushers, bikers, former prostitutes, and straight church kids are radiating the love of Jesus through smiles, testimonies, and Scripture. They talk about Jesus to the thousands of nomadic young people wandering on streets and beaches, to the teens in churches, and to adults in homes and bars.

The Jesus kids are everywhere. They meet for Bible studies in the basements of suburban homes — to the amazement of parents, who watch forty of their son's friends jam into the rooms.

"I could understand their trying a little marijuana," one mother exclaimed, "but this . . . !"

Old houses and storefronts are becoming Jesus teen centers with hundreds squeezing in. The Jesus kids fellowship together in coffee houses, pray in communes with tearful concern for the lost, and, with well-thumbed Bibles, teach one another about the Christian faith.

They are a generation that speaks honestly about personal feelings, and they don't hold back. They ask one another for prayer, embrace one another in sensitive Christian love, and listen eagerly to the teachings of an "elder" who may be only nineteen years old himself. And they gladly testify to the experience of God in their lives.

"The Lord radically changed my life," said Marty, the editor of a Jesus newspaper, "and he changed the lives of a few other brothers too. So we decided to tell as many people as possible that Jesus is the way. Our group grew from five to about three hundred spiritually reborn people who can now share the answer to drugs, hangups, frustration, and empty head games."

In Sacramento, Jesus marches have drawn eight thousand "God liberated people." In the overflowing Hollywood Jesus rallies, not their words or their songs but the happiness in their faces convinces the curious spectators that something real is happening in the lives of these young people.

"They have been liberated, set free," as one Jesus kid put it, "by simply letting the Prince of Peace into their hearts."

Another new convert added, "When I met these Christians, I couldn't believe it. I was stoned on grass; they were stoned on God."

Middle-aged adults with suits and ties and tailored dresses feel uneasy when one hundred, long-haired, barefooted, bearded, beaded hippies come into their church and sit on the floor for a Wednesday night prayer meeting. When the Bible teaching starts, the kids are intensely involved.

"Amen!" they shout.

"Heavy, man!" when the deep meaning of a verse is explained.

The adults squirm, and then anger begins to build up inside when their silent prayers are interrupted by many voices praying out loud, praising God, and petitioning with tearful emotion.

It's a little unnerving for the man who has been a Christian for many years to have a freaky looking youth ask him to explain the meaning of a passage of Scripture and not to know how to do it. For adults who have taken the Bible for granted, the desire of the young Christians to know the Scriptures seems fanatical. Also it is disturbing for a pastor to be asked by his church young people why he isn't out on the streets witnessing for Jesus instead of sitting behind his desk shuffling papers.

Is the Jesus movement simply the latest trip for young people who have tried everything else? They are, after all, kids. Most are in their teens, a few in their early twenties. They are impetuous, eager, enthusiastic, and committed. They want the world saved now!

These young people are also part of the youth subculture. The doubts about the older generation are still there; only now the churches instead of the establishment are the focus of their complaints. They believe intensely in Jesus Christ, but that belief has led some of them to take some strange theological trips. They need the church, but they don't think they need it or want it.

Yet they are taking the gospel of Christ into the streets, and there are some dimensions to the Jesus movement that the church is going to feel. The negative aspects of the Jesus move-

11

ment are real, but they can be corrected. The positive Christ-centered emphasis could bring about a new Great Awakening to the church and the world.

History will give the definite answers. Until then, each question and answer will have its supporters and detractors.

Is it real?

Will it last?

Is it Jesus Christ they've got, or are they on some emotional jag?

Ask an adult who has seen kids experimenting with sex and drugs while quoting Scripture, and he will tell you it's all phony.

Ask a pastor whose young people have left the church for a pentecostal Jesus meeting in a storefront, and he will say that the movement is shallow and one sided.

Ask a mother whose son dropped out of college in his last year to travel all over the country witnessing with other long-haired dropouts, and she will tell you that her son has lost his mind.

Ask an employer whose office girl quit without notice because "the Lord has called me to live in a commune," and he will shake his head in disgust.

But then talk to the father who says, "My son was into everything; I couldn't do anything with him. Now, he is loving and kind and helps around the house and prays before meals."

Talk to the mother who went to her daughter's prayer group to find out what was going on and stayed to ask Jesus Christ to come into her own life.

Ask the former member of the Hell's Angels, who once carried a sawed-off shotgun and is now an evangelist, if the Jesus trip is a fad.

Question Jack and Betty Cheetham, free-lance photographers who did a story on the Jesus kids (*Look*, February 9, 1971) and in the process gave their own hearts to Christ.

Talk to the lovely girl in a Jesus commune in Detroit. She sits quietly with an open Bible in her lap, the morning sunlight reflecting off her washed and combed brown hair.

"What do your parents say? Doesn't your mother object to your being here in this house with all these other people?"

She will smile and softly reply, "My mother knows what I used to be, before I met Jesus."

12

2

Jesus Puts It All Together

You see, the youth of today are increasingly alienated by what they perceive to be a cold and irrational environment. They are searching for a meaning, something to live for in an ugly world. Some try to change the world. Others develop mechanisms to cope with it. It is logical that the age-old favorite, religion, should experience a rebirth.

The Toronto Young Socialist, March, 1971.

"Do you see that girl over there?" A friend pointed toward a tall girl walking toward the prayer chapel in a Detroit Jesus center. "She had an $80-a-day habit before she came to Christ. When she was converted, she didn't even go through withdrawal."

Christopher Pike, twenty-one-year-old son of the late Episcopal Bishop James A. Pike, left behind marijuana, acid, and eastern religions when he came to Jesus. It was then, he said, that he knew he was a new creature.

"You want a trip, man?" an ex-biker asks a spaced-out kid. "Try Jesus Christ. Man, it'll really blow your mind."

The Jesus kids know what he is talking about. Most of them have been there before Jesus got hold of their messed-up lives and put them back together. A young Christian from Texas described what life had been like for him.

"I just traveled around the country getting into trouble. I used drugs and all the other stuff."

A former heroin pusher who now pushes Jesus said, "I felt at the end of the road."

The Jesus kids know that there are hundreds of thousands of

13

other young people at the end of the road who have not found Jesus. From Maine to California, young people take to the highways every summer. When fall comes, they are still out. They are part of the subculture, the alienated youth looking for a meaning to life that they didn't find at home. They crash with friends or sleep in the park. And they keep on hitchhiking — it doesn't matter where. Sometimes guys and girls travel together; sometimes they go alone. They stop wherever night finds them, not knowing if they will stay in that spot until the next morning or the next week.

Why do they do it? The street scene is a psychological jungle. It doesn't help them; it oppresses them. But they stay. When the visitor asks why, he gets various answers:

"I'm trying to put my head together," said a former machinist from Boston. "I've been on the streets about four months, but I won't go back until I get peace."

Question him about that peace, and he won't be able to describe what it is or how he will know when it comes.

"I'll just know," he says.

"At fifteen," says another one of the street people, "I was into drugs, sex, and lies. I would do anything. I would even hurt people. Here I am a part of this youth scene, supposedly wanting peace and happiness, and I'd do anything to come out on top."

A visitor walking down the streets of Denver, which the street kids call a "freak city," will be asked, "Have you got any spare change?"

The same thing happens in Berkeley. Every few feet a pedestrian will be asked for change. The reason that these kids beg is elementary; they are hungry! They have holes in their shoes and in their jeans. Even if they have a little money, it may be stolen. One hitchhiker lost his last few cents at knifepoint, and another wanderer had his backpack stolen while he slept. But they keep on wandering.

The police in most cities expect them. In some cities, especially in the West, public toilets and additional YMCA space are made ready in June for the influx.

Adults are amazed when they see these kids. They are not hoodlums or the derelicts that city policemen used to know. Many of them are well educated, soft-spoken, fresh-faced kids — guys still trying to grow a beard, and girls who left a home

14

where they had their own room and telephone. In Berkeley, 50 percent of the runaways who are under eighteen come from families with an income above ten thousand dollars per year, and over 80 percent of them are white. Many of the very young ones go back home, but the over eighteen year olds usually don't. They continue to drift.

A Berkeley city council committee reported in April, 1971, that the array of young people wandering the streets included remnants of the hippie scene, devotees of the drug culture (and those who sell to them), Hell's Angels types, political activists, runaways, and some artisan-craftsmen who tend to be self-supporting from the sale of their handwork.

In Berkeley, where many such street people "live," the Free Church, non-denominational, provides food for them and has a small army of hippie collectors out on the streets with tin cans to solicit donations for the free food program.

"We get to keep 20 percent of anything over five dollars," a young collector from Connecticut said. "That isn't as good as what you get collecting for the Free Clinic; they let you keep 30 percent.

The Free Clinic, operated by the Methodist Church, is open twenty-four hours a day offering medical, psychiatric, and drug crises service. Is it needed? The young collector shows his bandaged hand. He is one of fifty thousand patients who visited the Free Clinic in the last two years.

"They patched me up at the Free Clinic," he tells you. "That was the night I jumped out of the second-story window."

His story is not unusual. He explains that after midnight, people are looking either for a place to crash or for acid to get them through the night if they have no place to go.

"There are only so many places to sleep," he explains, "so if by 2 A.M. you haven't crashed, there is only one thing left — you go get a head of acid."

A person high on LSD can get through the night easily because he doesn't get bored. He can spend an hour contemplating a street light. In the morning, when he comes down, he will be jittery, pacing up and down, looking haggard. The ones who spent the night on acid are easy to identify.

Kids who have been around for a while will have a friend who can give them free LSD, but newcomers to the area who haven't yet made friends have to buy. The Free Clinic collector got his from a pusher. But when he told him that he didn't have any money, the pusher pulled a knife. That's when he went out the window.

They go to Berkeley, or Denver, or the mountains of Pennsylvania just to go someplace. They don't go looking for something; it's not that kind of journey. They are trying to beat the hassle of having to do or think about anything. That's why they leave home.

Inquire, and they will talk about the pressures that they felt at home:

"What are you going to do for a living?"

"Why don't you try to make something of yourself?"

"Look at you, your long hair, no shoes. What are people going to think?"

"It's time you got rid of those silly radical ideas and started fitting in. How do you think I got — "

The kids learn after a while that there is no point in discussing their problems with their parents. They just leave home, explaining, "It's always been a hassle with my parents. If I don't get into what they are into, they come down hard on me."

They go not so much to find something as to get away from the pressure. They don't plan where to go, or even think about tomorrow. They stand around, get a little music if there is someone playing (there usually is), sway with the beat if the music is African. They get stoned. Watch the girls play Frisbee. Rap with anyone who stops to talk — or do anything else that comes along.

"One night this guy came up to me," a kid sitting on a park bench tells you, "and said to me 'Hey, man, will you take care of my nymphomaniac girl friend tonight? I can't get any sleep.' So, I did, and it worked out fine for me, and he got the first good night's sleep he'd had in two weeks."

Outwardly, nothing seems to bother the street kids.

"How can you keep walking with holes in your shoes?"

"Oh, yeah," apparently noticing the holes for the first time, "they do have holes, don't they."

Conversation is easy. No one is in a hurry. There is lots of time, and there is no hassle.

"Are you going back to college?"

"I don't know."

"Are you going to get a job?"

"I don't know, whatever comes."

It's easy to talk about Jesus with these young people, but then it's easy to talk about the Age of Aquarius, or Mormonism, or the Mystical Teachings of the Fourth Way, or vegetarianism, or anything. Eastern religions are big; the occult, black-magic, devil worship is spreading. The wanderers will talk about anything; it may help them find meaning.

The Jesus kids know this kind of life, because so many came out of it themselves. Even the so-called "straight" kids, who never leave home or use LSD and always get good grades in school, have many of the same emotional struggles. The street people are everywhere because the street thinking is everywhere. And because the Jesus kids know the struggles from first-hand experience, they can communicate the message of Jesus Christ with real empathy.

"Jesus is real, man. He will change your life."

"Jesus is the bridge over troubled waters."

"Jesus really loves you."

"Jesus doesn't hassle you; he won't lay any legalistic trip on you."

Life on the streets is not all flowers and love anymore. Kids are flipping out; they are ending up in psychiatric wards or committing suicide. Young girls are going insane as they give themselves away in free love. Babies are born in public rest rooms. "Do your thing" sounded groovy once, but it has horrible effects. There are vegetables walking around who once were strong, young men and women.

"It's very sad," said a bearded elder of a Jesus commune. "They come to our Christian House, and some of them are so spaced out that they haven't got any mind left. There is a guy down in the park we call the "dot freak"! His mind is completely gone from drugs. Somebody must have told him that he could put a dot on his wrist with a felt pen and talk to it. That's what he does — wanders around talking to an ink dot on his wrist. There is no way to reach him now."

Those who make it back from the drug world have cause to praise God.

"The most amazing thing to me, and a real miracle, was not just my conversion," said a Denver ex-pusher, "but that I got my mind back. My mind was really gone; drugs will do that to you. When I came to Jesus, he healed my mind. I can read, and I can remember!"

There are a lot of sociological explanations offered for the wandering youth and their subculture. There are also some sociologists who try to explain why so many are turning to Jesus.

"The hippie movement is dead," they say. "The radical answers don't satisfy the kids anymore. Anti-establishment slogans don't rid the young people of all the drives and feelings that they have because they are products of the American culture and establishment. Even if they are opposed to middle-class values, most of them are still a part of the middle-class system, and they can't change that."

The sociologists go on to explain that the young people cannot wholeheartedly embrace philosophies or religions that are too divergent from their own background. A westerner cannot become immersed in Oriental thought; he needs something more familiar and comfortable. So, according to these social analysts, the young people turn to what has always been acceptable in America, Christianity. But they radicalize it by their strong emphasis on Jesus.

What is hard for the social analysts to understand and fit into their theory is that "straights" too, both young and old, are joining the Jesus movement. They also have a sense of identity as members of the body of Christ.

"It throws some people," the elder of one Jesus commune said, "because my hair is short and I don't wear unusual clothes, and I'm not rebelling against anything. They don't know how to explain my relationship to the Jesus movement, because I'm not a dissatified hippie."

The Jesus kids are not concerned about sociological explanations of the reason they love Jesus. Like the blind man healed by Jesus, they can say only, "Though I was blind, now I see." Once they wandered aimlessly seeking answers to questions about who they were, where they came from, where they were going, and what life was all about. They discovered the answers in Jesus. A new Christian named Will summed it up:

"He said that he is love — he is. He said that he would give life — he did. Jesus came to give peace to the world — I wish the world would let him."

The burden that the Jesus kids feel for others is real. There are tears of joy when someone confesses Jesus. They pray with agony for the kids they know on the streets. They love with a rescuing kind of love. Jesus is not just a nice idea. He is real, and they see him meeting people right where they are, on the streets.

Every testimony of conversion has a story behind it. When a new sister in Christ praises God for her conversion, it is not the "canned" testimony that is heard in so many churches. She was a lesbian before she gave her heart to Christ. She accepted Jesus one night when she had taken an overdose of barbiturates.

A guy described how his sister first turned him onto drugs. Then, he turned his little brother onto drugs. Then his sister told him about Jesus. Now he wants to lead his brother to Jesus.

Another young guy described his own unhappiness: "I had a good life — enough dope, some nice chicks, a good home, but there was something missing. Now, I love what God is making of me, and I want to give it to others."

The one with the red beard and the long hair sitting over in the corner of the crowded Jesus Bible study and prayer meeting came to Jesus from a life of wandering. He had been into everything — drugs, sex, and Satan worship.

"You never see him now without his Bible," his friends explain. "He doesn't just read it; he memorizes it." Red beard tells what it was like:

"It wasn't hard to get off drugs and sex, but my former friends had put the curse of Satan on me. I used to be into Satan with them, and it was hard to get away. It was getting me down because I was wearing myself out trying to fight what was too much for me. Alone, I was incapable of handling the power that Satan had over me. I had to trust the Lord because he had already overcome Satan. I knew that Satan couldn't win against him."

There are no raised eyebrows as he talks. Even to the middle-class suburban kids, who left their geometry and chemistry homework to attend the meeting, Satan is very real.

The Christians don't leave the streets. They go right back, but now they go with the Good News. They care for the street people with a seeking kind of care. They love them, but then so does Jesus.

Many of the street kids are outcasts from their homes. They are misfits. They are oppressed by drugs, sexual perversions, the police, society as a whole — and their own hangups. But most of all they feel the spiritual oppression of not having the inner warmth and peace that God designed them to need and want. For most of them, love (including the love of God) has been a teaching rather than an experience. They desperately hurt inside as they look for some meaning to life. The Jesus kids know and understand their feelings and their needs.

In almost every major city there are hot lines run by communes or Jesus centers, where twenty-four hours a day Jesus people man the constantly ringing telephones to minister to other young people who have lost themselves on drugs or who need some other kind of help. They catch people overdosed and get them to hospitals. They talk people down from a bad trip, convince others not to commit suicide, and pray with them to turn to Jesus. They advertise a thirty-second heroin cure with no withdrawal pains, and nobody laughs — they have seen it work.

Lyle Steenis, pastor of Bethel Tabernacle in North Redondo Beach, southwest of Los Angeles, has seen four thousand converted kids come off heroin in the last two years. As the March, 1971, issue of the Jesus newspaper *For Real* put it:

> God's Spirit changing lives! Changed lives giving evidence of receiving Christ. A complete turnabout. Throwing down on drugs. Cleaned-up insides evidencing this in cleaned-up outsides. Same faces, but radiating. Same bodies, same clothes, same hair, but clean for Jesus.

Ask them, "Are you happy?" and you will get a radiant, "Oh Wow, are you serious?"

You spot a young girl setting the table for the evening meal in a Jesus commune run by elders not much older than she is. She seems happy and contented, working and listening at the same time to a "brother" teaching the fulfillment of Old Testament prophecy to a Jewish-Christian girl, who is mending a pair of blue jeans. You learn that she has been living there for several months. She hasn't started high school yet, but a tutor comes to the house to help her meet the state's educational requirements.

"Is this any life for a fourteen-year-old girl who ought to be home with her parents?" you ask.

"Are you kidding?" a Christian brother replies. "She was riding with the Hell's Angels when she was twelve."

3

Fire in Their Souls

The leaders of the Jesus kids, though different in life-style and ministry from each other, have two things in common — a conviction that they are in the hands of God and a willingness to move and change direction as the Holy Spirit leads. Most of them give some evidence that they are chosen by God for their unique ministry to the young people. But a few give the impression that they are on a big ego trip, and in the Jesus kids they have found the following that they have always wanted.

One of the best known leaders of the Jesus kids is Arthur Blessitt, the just-turned-thirty minister of Sunset Strip in Hollywood, who is now opening a similar ministry among the topless bars and pornographic bookstores in New York's Times Square. This ordained Baptist minister, with hip clothes and drug-culture jargon, preaches a fundamental, hardhitting gospel to speed freaks, prostitutes, and barflies.

At His Place, a combination church and gospel night club, he fed free sandwiches and Kool-Aid to the Strip kids, preached once or twice every night, and saw hundreds respond to Jesus Christ.

"Toilet Services" followed many conversions as the kids crowded into the rest room to flush their pills and powders down the toilet. It was a tearful, moving experience as they destroyed the last of their drugs and turned for peace to Jesus.

Blessitt established the first His Place at 9109 Sunset Boulevard after a highly successful, if rather flamboyant, ministry among the tough night people of Elko, Nevada. The years at His Place were marred by continuous pressure from local businessmen who wanted him off the Strip and the police who hassled his kids to make him close up.

Strip businessmen lost money when Blessitt invaded their pornographic bookstores to shove gospel tracts between the pages of magazines.

Patrons had second thoughts about where they would spend the evening when they ran into Blessitt outside of their favorite nudie nightclub leading a gang of kids in a Jesus cheer ("Gimme a J; Gimme an E"; and so on).

Landlords, under pressure from the Strip businessmen, stopped renting to him with the excuse that their buildings were taken, although two of the four different buildings which Blessitt once rented for His Place are still vacant and padlocked.

Blessitt, in the words of those who know him, is an evangelist. He goes where others will not go. Next door to the building where he spent twenty-nine days on the sidewalk chained to a cross to protest his unfair eviction, and to convince someone to rent him another building, is a bar called "Big Als." The signs outside of "Big Als" tell the story of the neighborhood that Blessitt tried to reach for Jesus:

"Nude Sex Acts Nightly."

"Ten Popular Positions."

"Total Nude."

"Joe and His Sensuous Nymphs."

Some adults say that Blessitt is too pushy with his salvation message, but the kids love him. Whether he is on the Strip or is preaching in a local high school in Los Angeles or at a Jesus rally in Massachusetts, kids flock around him. To them, he is "the hip preacher," their "hippie chaplain."

The last building that Blessitt used before he moved from the Strip to Holloway drive is locked, and the terraced gardens in front are overgrown. Behind it, by a door marked "Sanctuary," is an old Chevrolet truck with outdated Pennsylvania plates and one flat tire. It looks like someone tried to strip it without moving the truck. There is psychedelic paint all over the body with signs lettered everywhere.

"Let's all get together."

"Turn on to Jesus."

"God is love."

"Are you saved?"

The rundown, decrepit truck just sits there now, a landmark to the ministry that once was, when thousands of young people thronged Sunset Strip and heard about Jesus.

The businesses which Blessitt fought are still there, with bold advertisements luring the middle-aged clientele. "Topless-Bottomless Dancers" provide entertainment for the cocktail crowd. Another sign calls hopeful dancers and spectators alike to "Amateur Nude Contests Every Sunday."

But the kids are gone. His Place is now offering daily Bible studies for businessmen and a nighttime walk-in center for people who want to know about Jesus. Blessitt left when the kids left, to follow the action, go where the street kids go, and preach Christ in the unusual places. If he is sensational, and knows how to attract attention, he is also the one that hundreds of formerly spaced-out kids point to as the man who introduced them to Jesus. They found a better life than they ever had known before Blessitt hit the Strip.

To the north of Los Angeles, another Jesus leader sits quietly on the sidewalk of Sproul Plaza at the Berkeley campus of the University of California. He is Jack Sparks, a bearded Ph.D. in blue denims, who edits a Jesus paper called *Right On*, leads Bible studies on the campus, and with love in his voice witnesses for Jesus. Unlike Blessitt, Sparks is quiet, not aggressive or pushy. The questioning kids come to him. He is available to the street people, always giving the impression that he is greatly interested in them and what they are thinking. He works well with small conversation groups.

Sparks has developed the Christian World Liberation Front, a movement of Jesus people who share Christ with other street kids. They pass out tracts at the university, operate a book table selling Bibles and Christian books, study the Bible together, baptize new converts in pools or the Pacific surf, worship together, and operate an increasing number of Jesus communes where they live together and strengthen one another in the faith.

Sparks gave up teaching at Colorado State and Penn State to write Bible correspondence courses for Campus Crusade for Christ. He left that movement in order to evangelize the street people at Berkeley. At first, kids worshiped in his home on Monday nights. When the number reached two hundred, the neighbors complained and forced him out. Rather than spend money fighting the issue in court, Sparks moved and the kids split up all over Berkeley establishing their witness in CWLF houses.

The same desire to communicate Christ that marks his personal witness characterizes Sparks' campus Bible studies. He teaches slowly, carefully explaining the text verse by verse. He brings in Old Testament passages wherever they help to explain the New Testament material. He moves back and forth between the testaments to show the fulfillment of prophetic messianic passages about Jesus.

Like Plymouth Brethren meetings, anyone can add to the lesson. Questions are answered immediately, with as much time given as is needed. Sparks is not concerned about the clock; he is concerned to communicate so that the kids understand.

What will Sparks do if the kids no longer come to Telegraph Avenue and Sproul Plaza? He shrugs and smiles, "God will find something else."

And so he goes about his business of listening intently to the kids who gather around to question him about Jesus.

On Hollywood's Fountain Avenue, not far from the Palladium, Duane Pederson, blond, lean, buckskin-shirted, zealous Jesus leader, runs the *Hollywood Free Paper* out of a house. He began the ministry of the *Free Paper* in 1969 with no journalism experience, and now he publishes the largest of the growing number of Jesus papers. The paper is now reproduced in twenty major cities, and Pederson hopes soon to reach a circulation of one million.

From running Jesus People training centers to conducting rallies at the Palladium, Duane Pederson is always on the move for Jesus. Although he tenderly answers his telephone with "Jesus loves you," he has little time to waste and pushes forcefully for Jesus.

The back page of one issue of his newspaper shows a guy running with a Bible in his hand. Underneath, it says, "Keep on Truckin' for Jesus." It's a good description of the philosophy he seems to hold.

Pederson is always at the forefront of Jesus gatherings, as the pictures in his paper show. The street rallies, the training meetings, and the marches have more meaning for him than the functions of the organized church. He feels that the church has kept the gospel inside its walls long enough; it needs to stop what it is doing and get out on the streets with the message of Jesus.

In every community where Jesus kids gather, leaders emerge. In Detroit, the Reverend George Bogle runs his House of Prayer, a combination commune, coffee house, and church. There he broadcasts every night from his own radio studio in the building. He preaches to the hundreds of young people who gather in the western decor coffee house on weekends and is the authority on God's Word for his people. A conversation with the people in his commune shows his influence:

"Brother George says. . . ."

"You should hear George preach."

"George believes. . . ."

Bogle is now opening another Jesus center in Pontiac, Michigan, similarly equipped with a radio studio. His followers eagerly travel with him to the new place in Pontiac to witness on the streets and help get the new work started.

Bogle tolerates no compromise with the hippie past of his converts. For him, the youth styles and counter-culture attitudes have to be left behind when a person becomes a Christian. The front window of his large storefront commune-church has pictures of his people before and after they accepted Jesus. Before, they are shown with long hair and beards, and they are dirty looking. The printed card beneath their pictures indicates that they were drug addicts or in trouble with the law. The new set of pictures, taken after accepting Jesus, shows them clean shaven with short hair and working as preachers or missionaries.

Some people became leaders of the Jesus kids just because they started Bible studies in their homes and the neighborhood kids kept coming in increasing numbers. Others sought the leadership more aggressively by quitting their jobs, moving into a particular area, and starting a house or storefront center where they held Bible studies and prayer meetings; and they preached and witnessed on the streets. One Newton Falls, Ohio, man started preaching in a barn. His youthful congregation kept growing until now there are hundreds of kids who are spreading the gospel in the Youngstown area.

One man who seems inclined to want to build a permanent

25

religious organization from the Jesus movement is Dr. Victor Paul Wierwille. This fifty-three-year-old founder of "The Way" program is developing a following among young people across the country and, he claims, in other parts of the world including Sweden and Samoa. He told *Life* magazine reporter Jane Howard that his Bible course offers "The first pure and correct interpretation of the Word since the first century A.D." (*Life,* May 14, 1971). His program offers studies in "Christian Etiquette," "Biblical Aramaic," "Speaking in Tongues," and "How to Deal with Satan."

Recently, from The Way headquarters on his 150-acre Ohio farm, Dr. Wierwille mounted his raspberry-and-white Harley Davidson '74 motorcycle and rode to Rye, New York, where he convinced some of the Jesus kids there to join his group. Wearing Holy Spirit doves on his cuff links, tie clasp, lapel pin, and ring, he tells his listeners that nothing bad can happen while he is around because he is not believing that it will happen. He urges them to "ooze" goodness wherever they go.

Life pointed out that the proven success of his belief in tithing can be seen in his remodeled farmhouse with its sunken mosaic bathtub and his planned 5.3 million dollar building program to keep up with the expansion of The Way.

Famous or not, quiet or aggressive, all of the leaders of the Jesus kids come across to their followers as authoritative, and all stress the place of the Holy Spirit in their lives. And, most leaders tie the charismatic gifts of the Spirit, particularly glossalalia (speaking in tongues), to accepting Jesus Christ.

Every Jesus commune has its elders, men who govern the house and teach the Christians living there. When one elder has a difference of opinion with another, he probably will break away and start his own commune, taking a few followers with him. But the Jesus kids do not seem to mind. They feel that God uses every personality and gift.

Most of the Jesus kids hesitate to assert their own opinions about either the leadership of their commune or the Bible teaching. Ask the young people why they do not speak up (they always had an opinion about what their parents taught and did), and they will say, "We don't know enough yet. We are still new Christians." So, if an elder wants to be authoritative, he has a ready-made audience that will let him.

In a Nashville commune, Francisco, a nineteen-year-old elder who was born in Equador and raised in Atlanta, has been known to go around the room during a house meeting and tell the residents, one by one, how they have failed Jesus. The kids take it in silence, convinced that the chastening comes from God, who is using Francisco to set them straight.

Ralph Morrison, elder of Vinewood House in Detroit, has been accused of racism because of his criticism of black worshipers who punctuate Bible teaching with "Yes, well, all right," or "Yes, Amen!" In a meeting where Frank Majewski, a bearded barber who is considered "cool" by Detroit kids, preached for three and one-half hours, Morrison stood up and told the attentive worshipers:

"I tell you on the authority of Jesus Christ, you grieved the Spirit. There is nothing wrong in saying 'hallelujah' and 'praise God.' . . . But this [the responses of the black people] is the spirit of a fleshly trip." [1]

Tony and Susan Alamo run their Christian Foundation in Saugus, California, like an ancient religious order. The doctrinal teachings are dogmatically presented and memorized, and the kids from their group are sent out on the streets day and night to recruit more people for their meetings. They "witness for Jesus," but their talk about "Jesus" is so mixed up with the rapid fire invitation to their meetings that the person to whom they are talking usually cannot determine what it is that they are promoting.

In Albuquerque, the leaders of the Christian House put no emphasis on street witnessing. "We have enough to do just to keep the house going."

They seem to be content to sit in the warm New Mexico sun. A sign attached to the building advertises Saturday night "Conserts [sic] for Jesus," but the Saturday night visitor shouldn't be surprised if he finds the building locked and dark.

Some leaders of the Jesus kids take their positions seriously as a divine calling to be handled prayerfully. They are well aware that they have been entrusted with young lives and that they are responsible to God for properly building them up in the faith.

For others, leadership is an ego trip.

[1] The incident is reported by Hiley H. Ward in the "Detroit Free Press."

Only the results of their ministries can verify the calling of each one, for all claim that they are called of God, that their authority to teach and admonish the young Christians is God given, and that their own wills have been surrendered to the control of the Holy Spirit.

In most cases the leaders are determining their authority for instruction from the Bible, and their teaching about Christian discipleship is scripturally based. In a few instances, the leaders are finding Scripture to support what they have already decided they want. The fortunate young Christians are taught to measure their leaders' teachings against the Bible, to make sure that they are correct. But some young people, particularly the not-too-well educated, have trouble distinguishing between the teachings of God and the teachings of their leaders.

A new generation of Christians has brought forth a new generation of leaders. Some are as zealous for God as the early Christian disciples. Others seem to have found a new way to satisfy their own emotional needs. As the movement spreads, it can be expected that there will be many more leaders coming along to teach the Jesus kids. One thing seems certain: All will be convinced that they have the fire of the Holy Spirit in their souls.

With new leadership, it is inevitable that many new ways will be developed to dramatize the gospel. The leaders, who speak of making Jesus known throughout the entire world within the next ten years, know that many new forms of communication will be necessary to accomplish that goal.

Already the trend has started. The Jesus kids are presenting a multimedia salvation message.

4

Multimedia Salvation Message

Light, color, and sound all vie for the attention of the young. Strobe lights flicker, blacklight illumines painted walls and painted faces. Phosphorous glows, candles give off colored flame, and incense fills the rooms where the youth subculture gathers to smoke marijuana or shoot heroin. Kaleidoscopic shapes move and swirl on the walls and ceilings. Pictures flash from projectors. Films with double exposures play off ceilings or large balloons.

Today is a multimedia age, and to reach their generation the Jesus kids have a multimedia message of salvation. The old-fashioned monologue in flowery language presented to a seated immovable congregation from the protection of a pulpit will not work for a swinging generation.

Jesus festivals draw thousands. Jesus marches climax spiritual revolution days. Posters in vivid colors line the walls of communes, the suburban, well-furnished bedrooms of the straight kids, and the school lockers of children.

"All power through Jesus."

"You have a lot to live; Jesus has a lot to give."

"Jesus is the Liberator."

"God's Speed Doesn't Kill."

Dashboard signs read: "If you hear a trumpet blast, grab the wheel. The driver has an appointment to meet Jesus."

Bumper stickers in day-glo colors are pasted on Jesus cars.

"Have a nice forever."

"Repent; boycott Hell."

"Honk if you love Jesus."

"Join God's forever family."

"I'm high on the love of Jesus."

"Love your enemy; it will drive him crazy."

And buttons saying "Have a nice forever" or showing a hand with the index finger pointing skyward in the "Jesus is the One Way" sign, are worn on shirts and jackets.

A Jesus motorcycle has a large cross built onto the back. It lights up when the brakes are applied.

"Jesus Saves" is stitched on the seat of a pair of blue jeans. Woven wire crosses dangle from pieces of leather hung around the necks of boys and girls alike. "Smile, God loves you" may be sewn anywhere on any piece of clothing. A picture of the head of Christ or the "One Way" sign may fill the back of a man's shirt.

The "All Saved Freak Band" plays at a Jesus rally in Philadelphia's Fairmount Park.

If to the adult generation this multimedia presentation of the holy work of God is flamboyant, indeed almost garish, it does attract attention. It's a conversation starter, offering a chance to ask, "Do you know Jesus?"

As the Jesus movement spreads, so does the amount and type of Jesus material. Jesus posters and fliers appear on college campuses and city streets. Jesus kids from different communes or teen centers join one another to pass out literature about any coming Jesus meeting; it doesn't have to be their own. As far as the kids are concerned, no one is building up a particular group. Jesus is to be lifted up; that is all that matters. They want their friends to meet Jesus, and they will use any kind of media presentation to get the job done.

Inter-Varsity Christian Fellowship sponsors "Twenty One Hundred," a multimedia presentation of the Christian message. It was developed by Eric Miller, who (as an intern from Fuller Theological Seminary) created the battery of slides, movie projectors, lighting effects, and stereophonic sound in rock and soul music for African Enterprises in Nairobi, Kenya. Thousands of college young people are experiencing this presentation of the feelings of man in his alienation from other men, his environment, himself, and God.

The American Bible Society has published Luke's account of the resurrection of Jesus in *The New Testament in Today's*

English Version on glossy psychedelic paper. The Jesus kids pass it out on the streets.

The Christian World Liberation Front has published *Letters to Street Christians,* a paraphrase of Ephesians, First John, and James in hip street language.

> Don't get hooked on the ego-tripping world system. Anybody who loves that system doesn't really love God. For this whole gig — the craze for sex, the desire to have everything that looks good, and the false security of believing you can take care of yourself — doesn't come from our Father, but from the evil world system itself. That world system is going to be gone some day, and, along with it, all desire for what it has to offer; but anyone who follows God's plan for his life will live forever. (Dig it! This whole plastic bag is exactly what Jesus liberated us from.)
>
> Paraphrase of 1 John 2:15-17
> From *Letters to Street Christians*
> (Grand Rapids: Zondervan Publishing House, 1971)

The Hebrew Christian Fellowship has produced colored fliers with eye-catching titles designed to introduce the street Jews to Jesus Christ. "Is it true Jews don't believe in Jesus?" "If being born hasn't given you much satisfaction, try being born again"; "Kosher pigs"; and "Christmas is a Jewish holiday," are some of the titles passed out to the increasing number of Jewish young people who are interested in hearing about Jesus.

A 1968 survey showed that 30 percent of the hippies in San Francisco were Jewish. The Reverend Martin Rosen, minister of the Bar Shalom Hebrew Christian Fellowship, says that approximately two hundred Jewish young people in the Bay Area have come to Christ in the past two years, most of them street people.

The life story of former drug users Jeff and Carrie Buddington, reprinted from *Guideposts,* May, 1970, is passed out on the streets and displayed for free pickup by visitors in Jesus communes and teen Jesus centers. Every Jesus kid has bundles of tracts, which he hands out wherever he goes. Most are Bible tracts with catchy titles and provocative opening statements that lead the reader to investigate the message about Jesus printed inside. "What the Bible Says About Hippies," "Those Christian Cats Keep Bugging Me," "The Bible is Inconsistent and Contra-

31

dictory." A booklet showing a little boy leaning against a tene-
ment wall in a filthy alley begins, "If you were God . . ." and
leads into a short Bible study course on the sin of man.

Entire tabloid pages in Jesus newspapers are given over to
the plan of salvation with bold pictures of love hitting the
earth like an arrow, man separated from the light of God by a
chasm, the cross serving as a bridge to God, and everything
culminating in freedom. The presentation is simple, designed
for the person who is foggy on drugs, in order to show him the
way to salvation.

But the same kids who distribute the simple tracts and plan
of salvation also reach out to the intellectuals. On college campuses the Jesus people promote Dr. Myron S. Augsburger's lec-
ture "The Claims of Christ"; Dr. Paul Krishna, the former
Hindu, speaking on "The Appeal of Eastern Mysticism"; Dr.
David Breese, "Discover Your Destiny"; and Dr. Clark Pinnock
on the subject "Biblical Infallibility." The Jesus kids do not
ignore the intellectual seeker, but neither do they assume that
everyone can handle it. Most of the time they use the startling
poster and the eye-catching tract to catch the attention of the
street kids.

Even the people who use the old-fashioned method of preaching have a drawing testimony that is unusual enough to catch
the young people's attention.

"Holy Hubert," a middle-aged man who has been a regular
preacher on Berkeley's Free Speech platform, is known by Jesus
people and radicals alike in the three western coastal states. In
the past four and one-half years, Berkeley's radicals have beaten
him up and sent him to the hospital twelve times. On at least
two occasions he went to the city jail and bailed out the guys
who beat him up. That kind of turning the other cheek and
loving your enemy communicates to the street kids and wins
their attention for a gospel sermon.

Wesley Smith, a traveling evangelist who speaks at Jesus rallies
and in churches, was fired from his school teaching position for
witnessing in school and having Jesus Bible studies in rented
buildings. Since 1965 he has not held a job, but has traveled,
preached, and led Bible studies around the country. He plans
soon to build a Bible school in Florida to train the Jesus kids in
Bible and the charismatic gifts. The kids are impressed because

here is a man who has gotten away from the daily nine-to-five routine. They listen to him because he talks of a faith and trust in the Lord that they see him practicing. When he talks about people being converted from drugs, they are people he knows. When he speaks of challenging street kids to trust Jesus, everybody knows that he has been out on the streets himself witnessing to the kids.

When Arthur Blessitt arrives in a city to preach at an outdoor rally, he does not bring a sermon but the message "Jesus loves you." He is advertised as the one who dramatically drew the attention of the press by traveling across the country carrying a cross and being chained to a cross on Sunset Boulevard. Until he moved to New York, he was the "minister of Sunset Strip." There he witnessed to the night people, talked down kids on bad trips, and almost lost his two-year-old son, Joel, who swallowed a pill containing speed and downers that a street kid dropped on the floor of His Place. His experiences and his non-preacher garb make him attractive to the kids, and they flock to hear him preach.

When CWLF leader Jack Sparks conducts a Bible study or preaches, people know that he has had hundreds of street kids in his home, gave up a regular paycheck to witness to them, and has been forced out of the neighborhood where he lived because of his freaky friends. Even non-Christians are impressed by a man who baptizes people in a public fountain.

In every case the people who preach to the Jesus kids have something to commend them besides their ability to sermonize. Their lives are as eye-catching as the material that they distribute.

When twenty-seven-year-old Ken Christie takes his gospel night club act into the bars, he often preaches as long as twenty minutes to the drinking crowd about their need to accept Jesus Christ as Savior. He sings "Cling to Jesus," "Sweet Jesus, Smile on Me," and "Have You Been to Jesus?" in Bobbie's Lounge on Detroit's Northwest side. The manager says Christie has been good for business.

But the most eye-catching material and binding force of the Jesus movement is the ever growing number of Jesus newspapers. The papers are springing up all over the country, each with a different format, but all like tabloid tracts reaching out to the seeking youth generation and carrying biblical material to build new believers in the faith.

When David Abraham accepted Jesus Christ on Haight Street in San Francisco, he gave all of the publishing rights to his paper, the *Oracle,* to the Jesus people of Harvest House in the Haight-Ashbury district. The paper had been a psychedelic monthly newspaper that featured sex, drugs, eastern religions, and explicit photographs.

A few months later, the *Oracle* was on the streets again, this time as a Jesus newspaper. The small-type tabloid is jammed with study material that shows the difference between Jesus Christ and other religions, and offers biblical instructional material for the Christians. It has little art work, except for the borders, and has been printed with purple ink. It is what the Jesus kids call a "heavy" paper because it probes into some of the deep theological concepts of the Christian faith.

The *Hollywood Free Paper,* which has the largest circulation of all of the Jesus newspapers (400,000 and growing) is also a tabloid. Unlike the *Oracle* it has a lot of white space, large type, and art work made with broad-point pens. It is modeled after the *Los Angeles Free Press,* a secular underground newspaper. It carries a simple gospel message, usually in short sentences, advertises Jesus rallies and celebrations, and encourages people to take advantage of the Jesus people training programs such as those held at the Hollywood YMCA.

Taking an idea from the personal sex ads in the *Los Angeles Free Press,* the *Hollywood Free Paper* runs ads for Jesus centers, rap sessions, Bible studies, and coffee-house programs all over the United States and Canada. Street people who pick up the paper can easily find the listings of the Jesus meetings nearest them.

Like most of the other Jesus papers, the *Hollywood Free Paper* is distributed free on the streets and campuses with a small charge for people who want it delivered. Bulk copies cost a few cents per copy, but the paper advertises: "If you don't have any 'bread,' that's cool — come on down and pick some up anyway."

CWLF's newspaper *Right On* has a circulation of about 65,000. Similar in format to the *Oracle,* it regularly features a front-page inset called "Let's get one thing straight," which usually begins: " 'Right On' has one line for the people: God's Unique Son, Jesus, holds the key to the solution of any basic human problem you can suggest."

Right On concentrates its cartoons and testimonies on material for the drug users, occult followers, and the radical left. It began publication in a form that satirized the *Berkeley Barb,* but now it has its own style. (A collection of excerpts from *Right On* has been published under the title *The Street People* by Judson Press, 1971.)

There are many other Jesus newspapers, most of them with circulations exceeding the *Los Angeles Free Press,* the largest of the underground secular newspapers. *Together,* published by the New Community in Christ in Kenmore, New York; the *Maranatha Free Paper,* of Vancouver, British Columbia; *Truth,* published in Spokane, Washington, are a few of the popular Jesus papers. A Jesus News Service International has been organized in the Berkeley area to link the papers together and supply the breaking news of the Jesus movement to all of them.

Jesus people are freewheeling and not afraid to try anything that will promote the gospel and give them an opening to share Jesus Christ with someone. But they do become offended when interests with a secular leaning try to move in on the Jesus scene.

Pop music like "Spirit in the Sky," "Jesus Is a Soul, Man," and "Jesus Christ Superstar" is seen by many Jesus people as a non-Christocentric offering to kids to capitalize on their interest in Jesus but not to offer them the true Christ. The Jesus kids have Jesus music, but it has not been produced commercially. Singer Larry Norman has written that there has not been any real Jesus music done by the commercial interests.

Commercialism has shown up in other ways too.

Dave Balsiger, former staff member at Melodyland Center in Anaheim, has created a Jesus watch, like the Spiro Agnew watch. It has a figure like Casper the Ghost on the face pointing its hands to the time, and the words "Jesus People" printed on it. Supposedly, the watch is a conversation starter to make witnessing easier, but to many of the Jesus kids it is a gimmick like the Jesus sweatshirts and other commercialized paraphernalia.

The multimedia salvation message developed by the Jesus kids may have aroused persons with commercial interests, who see new ways to make a dollar, but their expression of the message is showing the church that there is more than one way to present the gospel message. The church will need more than a sermon to hold kids who have been on the streets promoting Jesus with creative materials.

But the Jesus movement is not all street witnessing, gospel rock concerts, and day-glo posters. The Jesus kids also feel a vital need for prayer, Bible study, and Christian fellowship — the kind that satisfies the deep spiritual and emotional needs of people. There is also the need for a place to live while they are serving the Lord and growing in their newfound faith.

The Jesus kids have found their answer, not in churches or with their parents, but in one of the most distinctive aspects of the Christian youth scene — the Jesus communes.

5

The Jesus Communes

It is not surprising to many that a generation which sought security in personal wealth and which stressed houses and things as goals should produce offspring who rebel and seek a life-style of their own based on a different value system. Rebellion has always been characteristic of the young. Every generation of adults has learned to smile at the enthusiastic teenagers who have "found the truth" and to tolerate their criticism of the older generation with a "wait until you have teenagers of your own" attitude.

But what has been distressing to the parents of this generation is the intensity of feeling among the young in their reactions to the establishment. The young have created their own counter-culture. This subculture, which is a product of the hippie movement combined with the dreams of the flower children, is now permeating and influencing all strata of society. The changes by the youth are shocking to adults when these changes upset an established value system.

Historians who know something of the French Bouzingo youth movement in the 1830's see a parallel to today. Those youth wore their own style of clothes, sometimes tried to shock adults by going nude in the streets, and protested against the materialism of their parents. They also used drugs, as did the young people during the decline and fall of Rome when faith in the establishment was lost.

The cool materialism of adults, the seeming inability of many parents to show love to their children and to be open on a feeling level even with each other, has caused a hunger for community in the young. Parents, shocked at "free love," have seldom bothered to analyze the yearning for love that has driven so many young to try the only method they knew to try to find it.

The hippie communes are attempts to reestablish human community with values on the person, rather than on what the person does or can produce. They became popular in the 1960's, particularly among the more philosophically radical youth. But they too lacked the one ingredient that was so much wanted — love.

Love — not humanly produced love, which is dependent upon human will alone, but love flowing to and through people from God — was the factor that the hippie communes did not have. So, while such communes are quickly becoming a phenomenon of the past, the Jesus communes, or New Testament Christian communities, are growing.

The Jesus kids who are moving into communes are still the products of their age and upbringing. Their backgrounds and longings are the same as their hippie contemporaries. Their conversion to Christ could not change the environment that made them a part of the youth subculture. The same social influences, the same home life, the same hunger for love and identity which produced the rest of their generation produced them.

But in Christ they have discovered the missing part. The love they have found is greater than the love they could generate within themselves. They are loved by God, and they are loved by other "brothers" and "sisters" in Christ, who give them the family identity that they have needed. Feeling redeemed and loved, and longing for others to know their Savior, the kids in the New Testament communities have goals and drives that satisfy the inner person. Because they are based on the kind of genuine love and concern that characterized the fellowship of the first-century believers, the Jesus communes are spreading all over the country. Kids are finding the love of God and the love of people at the same time, and the joy of it is overwhelming.

One of the first Christian communes was the House of Acts, which started in the mid-1960's in Novato, California. It attracted so many people that the commune idea among Christians quickly spread. In Haight-Ashbury the Soul Inn and Clayton House opened, and in Berkeley God's Love was soon in operation. Since then communes have been established all over the country. One compilation puts the number at six hundred, but no one can be sure because they open and close and change locations very rapidly.

The signs on the front door, "One Way" or John 3:16 printed in full, tell a visitor that he is at a Jesus house. Rarely are there signs out front. The house looks like any other in the neighborhood to someone walking past. Inside, more signs hang on the walls telling of the love of God in Christ. Scripture verses are tacked on bulletin boards or stuck in mirrors. Bibles, tracts, and devotional material are on tables where they can be easily picked up for study. There are usually no television sets or record players in the houses. The Jesus kids have neither the time nor the money for those.

Anti-war and anti-establishment posters, which cover the walls of the hippie communes, are missing in the Jesus houses. There are strict rules about no drugs, alcohol, or swearing. Everyone understands that the relationship between the "brothers" and "sisters" is to be kept just that — brotherly and sisterly.

"There isn't any problem," explained one young man, "when you follow the Book and follow Jesus."

Most houses have between six and fifteen residents, depending on the number of rooms in the building. The men usually outnumber the women, and the "elders" of the houses are always men. The kids are conscious of the family relationship, enjoying one another's company, laughing and working together, but always allowing a person to be alone when he feels the need. There is very little stress. The elders have the final word in house decisions; and with the exception of an occasional authority figure, the elders are generally like big brothers.

A day in a Christian commune usually begins about 10:00 A.M., with a prayer meeting and Bible study. The rest of the morning is devoted to cleaning, and with few exceptions the Christian communes are spotless. Furniture is secondhand, the walls may be poorly painted, but the house will be clean. Household duties are divided. The women do the cooking, sewing, and cleaning; and the men do the yard work, make repairs, and take the responsibility for the administration of the house. Jesus people take their responsibilities seriously, and there seems to be little rancor over the distribution of work.

The afternoons are spent by the men witnessing on the streets, passing out tracts in a shopping center, or talking to their non-Christian friends about Jesus. Only occasionally do the women go out on the streets to witness, and then usually with a male escort. Some of the women may have a ministry to nursing homes or with children.

The evenings are spent either in more street witnessing, or in Bible studies, prayer meetings, and neighborhood ministries in private homes or coffee houses. Usually the night meetings will go very late, particularly the week-end coffee-house ministries with an evangelistic thrust. A Jesus kid described how his group works at a coffee house. "We present the gospel through music, personal evangelism, and rapping on the stage. Usually over 150 people come each night that it is open, and around 200 on the Bible study nights."

Few commune residents hold regular jobs. They feel that they must give all of their time to growing as a Christian and introducing other people to Jesus. There isn't time to work at a secular job. When Christ is offered, there has to be a flow between the two people that begins to bring healing and hope. This relationship is costly in time. It demands that a person listen. It requires sensitivity. A person coming off drugs, or even one who is "clean," needs counsel that is gentle and slow. So they feel it is a full-time job to be a good witness for Jesus.

The Jesus kids are not lazy. They work much more than eight hours each day. But they don't want to spend good working time just earning a paycheck.

Neighbors have confessed that they thought of selling their house when "those long-haired freaks rented the place next door."

Tom, the elder of a commune in Detroit's Northwest section, has put so many hours into yard work and painting that his neighbors have changed their minds. The "normal" family that rented the house before let it run down until it was in terrible shape. Tom and his "family" now have the house looking better than it has in years.

"It blows their minds," said Tom. "Hippie types are supposed to be slovenly."

He hopes that the repair work on the house will cause some of his neighbors to listen to what he has to say about Jesus.

Some communes do have a ministry in their neighborhoods. The Jesus kids use their Bible knowledge to lead home Bible studies and fellowship meetings in the community. Neighbors come, sometimes out of curiosity, more often at the urging of their teenage children.

Elders, who may have been Christians themselves only a year, often will be able to answer biblical questions that have puzzled many older church people for years. Many have memorized more Scripture in a few months than some churchmen have learned in their lifetimes. And they know what they have memorized. When asked a question, the youthful leaders will flip quickly through their Bibles to one passage after another that relates to the question and they will be able to explain how the passages all fit together. This ability comes from spending hours with the Book. They have a desire to know God's Word well, and they work at it.

Some Jesus kids live in communes only a short time, either because they are traveling through or because they are using the house for a spiritual retreat. But others stay a long time. Few will admit to knowing how long they will stay. They will leave, they say, when God directs them to leave.

Kids live in the communes because they need each other. There is comfort in having people around who care about you. The temptation to go back on drugs is much stronger for the person who tries to live the Christian life alone. Kids know that drugs gave them release from pressure before they accepted Jesus. If they did not have their Christian brothers and sisters to talk to and pray with, they likely would try drugs again. They are all struggling together, so they do not judge one another. As brothers and sisters, they are supportive of one another.

They would not go out on the streets to witness as much if they were living alone either. They know that they inspire each other. It only takes one person to say, "Let's go pass out tracts tonight," to get the rest moving.

At 10:30 one morning, a resident of one commune came hurrying down the stairs, still wiping the shaving cream off of his face.

"I heard someone say that a carload is getting ready to go out."

"They're leaving in a few minutes," a brother replied.

"Tell them to wait for me," he called out as he ran upstairs to get a shirt.

Communes are busy places. "There are now fifteen full-time residents with many guests coming in all the time for fellowship, help, and spiritual guidance," an elder explained. And, because the commune is a seven-day-a-week Christian experience, there is always help for those who come.

There is only one limitation to the Christian hospitality of the Jesus kids. If someone comes into their house with drugs, he is asked to leave. Always the person is given the gospel message, but he is not allowed to stay around unless he gives up his drugs. This response seems cruel to the outsider, almost opposite from the love that the Jesus kids talk about, until one understands the power of drugs to these kids. To admit drugs is like putting a bottle in front of a former alcoholic, and the Jesus kids will not let themselves be tempted.

"I know it sounds hard and even narrow," a brother explained, "but most of us have been that route and we can't compromise, even to having the junk around while we rap about Jesus."

Usually, when a Jesus commune starts to get run down, there is a spiritual problem behind it. Either the kids have gone back to drugs, or they have begun to lose their desire to grow in the Lord, or the decline may be evidence that they never really knew Jesus — just words about him.

One house stopped witnessing, stopped cleaning, and the residents themselves were dirty. They would wander around during the day, sleep late, and rarely open their doors to visitors. When a utility company representative called them to ask for payment on their past due bill, the elder cursed her.

"Those Jesus kids have just baptized their old habits," complained a Southern Baptist woman when she encountered drugs and free sex in a so-called Jesus commune.

Another Southern Baptist had a similar experience. He said, "They asked to stay a few days. There were only a few so we let them use our building. A month later when we finally drove them out, there were thirty of them in there."

"We've got to expect that some people will call themselves

followers of Jesus," a leader of the Jesus kids explained. "For them it's an 'in' thing. But they don't know Jesus, and they won't be around when it starts to get tough to be a Christian."

Most communes have established their credentials with the community.

"This used to be a hippie hangout, and a guy was killed upstairs. Some say he shot himself." An older man likes to tell that story to visitors who come to the combination commune and teen center. It is his way of expressing his pleasure for what the kids are doing. He was in the commune getting coffee ready for the evening Bible study. He is excited about the Jesus kids and said he spent almost every evening helping them with their work.

"Now," he continued, "the police come in here to have coffee and donuts. The police are really happy that *we* took over this house."

In another city, the police bring delinquents to the Jesus house. "They figure that if the kids haven't done anything too bad but might be on the road to bigger trouble, we might be able to help them," explained a pleased brother.

Nashville businessmen would not give financial support to the 23rd Psalm, a commune on Seventeenth Street, until they first questioned the police and received a favorable report of their work.

"Police problems!" exclaimed an elder in still another city, "Not at all. They're glad that we're helping out with the teen-age runaways. The kids come in here looking for a place to sleep, and we try to convince them that they should go home. When they are ready, we call the police."

He produced a letter of commendation from the municipal police chief.

"Why don't you frame that letter and hang it up?" an uninformed visitor suggests.

"Then the kids wouldn't come in here at all! They'd be certain we were going to turn them in."

The relationship with the police is not the same in the non-Christian communes. In a mountain community twenty-five miles west of Boulder, Colorado, the local store has a sign out front that says "One hippie at a time in the store." Their reputation for stealing is well established. Many carry knives and guns and live off of the land. Hippies who once established what they thought would be an ideal community based on peace and justice are now fighting among themselves and drifting apart.

"Oh, it's a lot quieter here now," said an Albuquerque resident. "You can tell the hippies are leaving because there are fewer gunshots in the night. Vigilante groups are no longer trying to force them out."

Even the non-Christian communes that have some philosophical or ethical value system to bind them together are finding it difficult to continue. They can't get others who come in to accept their concept of what a community should be. Spectators come in "just to see what a commune is like." They are bored or come looking for drugs. One former resident described what it was like:

"It came down to a few of us who took care of the place and worked in the craft shop while the rest just ate the food and did nothing. They thought it was a great trip to come in here and look for someone to sleep with."

Some of these groups that still hope to continue as a commune with a purpose are moving away from the heavily populated areas to find solitude in remote mountain or desert areas. But many of the non-Christian communes are splitting up.

At a commune in Berkeley, based on a religious belief in "Alan the Cosmic Messiah," even the teachings of their spiritual leader do not keep the members from arguing about whose job it is to work in the kitchen that day.

One Sunday morning, at a "family" worship service, the residents of this commune found themselves thinking more about the operation of their restaurant than their spiritual beliefs. The restaurant, where they sell only organically grown foods, is supposed to be their means of showing the world that there is a better way to live. The original plan was that each resident would share in the work of the restaurant; the income would enable them to live as a family; and their customers would see by their happiness that in their "messiah" they have the answers to a world that is confused about values. To them, this world is artificial — a shadow of the "real" cosmic world of love, peace, and mutual sharing. In the "real" world, no one grasps for things of his own; everyone shares equally.

But, their dream about living in the "real" world is not working out. They are having trouble being happy enough to convince their customers that they really have something good to offer. Their constant fussing over who does what and how to make equal work loads keeps them from having the impact that they want to have on the people who come into the restaurant.

A guy and a girl from Michigan, visiting the Berkeley commune for ideas for a similar commune in the Upper Peninsula, admitted that they have the same problems in their group. They have four people who want to start a commune, but they cannot agree on how to start it. They also have different opinions (depending on their personal vocational leanings) about what to do for the support of their commune when it gets started.

For most hippies, communal living is part of a larger search for a better world system than they see around them. Neither society as a whole nor their families have given them any hope that human relationships based on love and understanding can be brought into a system that "loves things and uses people." The commune is a withdrawal from what they consider to be a messed-up social order and an attempt to create something better. But they are finding it to be a lost cause. The basic problem, they are learning, is not the world order but the people who make up the world order. Those same people are in their communes.

The Christian communes, on the other hand, have a binding concept of community in Jesus Christ. This commitment takes the leadership out of the realm of their own ideas and relates it to the One who called them into community. They serve Christ, not a concept.

Even when a strong dominating leader becomes an elder, the Jesus kids who choose to live in the commune do so because of a loyalty to Christ and a caring for each other. A poor leader can still be a teacher for people who are praying to be taught through that leader. The seeds of dissent which show up in a hippie commune do not grow in a Jesus commune when the real authority for each one is Christ.

Whereas the hippie commune leaders have to struggle to keep the original purpose of their community before their residents, Christ is the center of the Christian commune. No one has to remind another about that because Christ is first of all the center of their own individual lives. The Jesus kids come together because of their oneness in him, not to create a oneness in him. They care for each other because they are a family, not because they are under pressure to prove something to the world. In fact, the Jesus kids are really quite relaxed about their family relationship, in much the same way that a natural family is relaxed. They don't try to be something; they just are.

To the uptight Christian adult who has to be always striving, the Jesus kids seem almost lackadaisical. They are not under pressure to build or become or do; they just enjoy being Christians by enjoying the Lord and each other. Their Bible studies are not the "we really should study the Bible more" variety known to the average Christian in the organized church. They want to study the Bible and worship together because of the enjoyment of it. And, if someone points out that they keep each other excited about it, they would admit that this is the reason they are in the commune.

Also, for the Jesus kids, witnessing is not the tyrannical "should" that it is for many Christian adults who feel guilty until they get up enough courage to talk to someone about trusting Christ. While the church evangelism committee is concerned about "how many souls did you win to Christ?" the kids in the Jesus commune see witnessing as God's work. They feel no pressure to win people just because it is the thing to do. They witness because they love people enough to want them to have the same peace and deliverance that they have. They know what the street kids are experiencing, because they know what they themselves went through. Their burden for the street kids is that they may know Jesus for what he can mean to them, not because as Christians they are "supposed" to witness. And knowing that God wants the street people to accept Christ, the Jesus kids go out with a sense of "God is with me." As a result, they come back to their family in the commune rejoicing not that "I won someone to Christ," but that "Wow, God has just brought a new one into his 'forever family.' "

To the Jesus kids, the commune is home, but it is not a perfect home. There is a weakness in its structure.

The weakness in the Jesus communes is not, as some adults imagine, in the concept of guys and girls, blacks and whites, living together. Their morality is generally well practiced and well proven.

The greatest weakness in the Jesus communes is that they are not true to life. The commune is a family of choice:

The kids live together because they *want* to.

They obey their elders because they *want* to.

Jesus is the head of the house, because they all *want* him to be. And, if there are tensions or conflicts, they can leave anytime they want to.

A natural family, the neighborhood, a city, a state, the nation are not always the "communities" that people would choose for themselves. Mature people know that they cannot live only with like-minded people, where they want to live, under the leadership of those they want for their leaders with everyone around them acknowledging Jesus. People cannot have only what they want, or leave a situation when something does not please them. Community demands that members stay and bend even when they do not feel like it. The Jesus kids have a luxury, which they will not have when they leave the commune.

Yet the communes are needed — especially for former drug users. It is a place of acceptance, where there is no hassle. A commune is just the retreat that is needed for the slow, drug-ruined mind trying to regain some balance. It is a place where former rebels learn to share with others in preparation for the giving required by society. People who are hungry for love find it in the safe, protective family that will not hurt or use them.

The Jesus commune is a Christian training center, a sensitivity group, a therapy program — and it works. It may be only a way station, but it is a necessary way station.

The communes are an experience in Christian fellowship. The kids, coming out of all types of backgrounds, are finding a family — in some cases for the first time.

Just as it costs money to keep every other family, it also costs money to maintain the Christian commune. Unlike many churches, with budgets, projected annual incomes, and every-member canvasses, the kids in the communes "trust the Lord." But those words mean something different to the Jesus kids than they do to the vocal churchman who says, "I don't think we should pledge. I think we should trust the Lord." To that churchman those words usually mean "I will give what I can after I take care of my own needs." The result is that he holds on to his own, calls it trust, when in fact God cannot trust him.

The Jesus kids are different. They live together and share together. There is no separate income for one while the rest go without. Everyone eats, or no one eats. Having pledged themselves to Christ, they have also pledged themselves to each other as a family; and no one in the family is told to "trust the Lord" while his brother has food on his plate.

"The Lord will provide" is not a pious phrase. To the Jesus kids it means what it is coming to mean to an increasing number of alert Christians: a genuine trust in God and a genuine commitment to each other in Christ. As one body, they learn to trust God to provide the needed "manna from heaven."

6

Manna from Heaven

They don't need the money that their parents would gladly give them, and they don't want the money that their parents wish they wanted. Most of the Jesus kids, like their hippie contemporaries, have always had money available. It does not hold the allure for them that it did for earlier generations who never had enough and resolved to "someday have financial security."

After he stopped pushing heroin and became a Christian, one of the Jesus kids took a job for a few weeks. "I worked just long enough to get a couple of shirts and a pair of pants," he said.

Lazy? He went on to explain that he quit so that he could devote all of his time to witnessing. He is going back to every person that he can find to whom he once sold heroin and tell them about Jesus Christ.

A blond twenty-year-old guy stopped for a moment and thought. Then he said, "If I had a part-time job where I could earn maybe one hundred dollars a month, that would take care of all my wants. Then I could spend the rest of my time doing what I'm doing right now." He was passing out tracts and witnessing to kids in Berkeley's Sproul Plaza.

In a company economy move, the boss called a young engineer into his office and explained that they would have to let him go.

"I was delighted," the engineer said. "My wife and I were praying about the job, and we took the dismissal as God's sign that we are to be full-time missionaries for Jesus."

Another college graduate, with a degree in Fisheries and Wildlife, is happy to be simply a "fisher of men." "We will stay here as long as the Lord wants us here; then we'll move on."

He and his wife feel called to travel around the country setting up Jesus centers and communes wherever there are Jesus kids who need help. "So far," he said, "we have been able to keep our old Ford running, and we don't need much to live."

The Jesus kids really don't need much to live. A secondhand bed in a commune, a patched pair of jeans, a jacket if the weather turns cold, and a pair of heavy walking shoes are enough. They don't need their own room or several changes of clothing, just a place to sleep. And their clothes are just right for establishing rapport with the street kids.

People can get by on plain food. The Jesus kids, many of whom grew up in homes with adequate food budgets, enjoy the simple stews and oatmeal of the communes. The Christian World Liberation Front has issued a booklet telling the kids how to eat a balanced diet on just seventy-nine cents a day.

Jesus house meetings include the practical prayers for existence, but always with the idea that if God does not want the commune to continue, the funds will not come in. A note from CWLF's Agape House states: "God has taken care of food this past week, and the bills were all paid. There is a continual need for food though. Pray for a means of getting insurance for the van and for support for the brothers." Most of the CWLF "staff" earn fifty dollars or less per month.

"Trusting the Lord" is the key, say the Jesus kids. Every Jesus center, commune, and coffee house has experienced the arrival of a check for the right amount just as bills have come due. The kids do trust, and they do get the money. They are experiencing a thrill that many of their parents ("You have to work for everything you get") have not experienced.

Occasionally a Jesus commune will run a business. The House of Life, in Kenmore, New York, has a construction company called "The Carpenter's Men." They do siding, roofing, and residential construction to provide for their needs.

As the Jesus kids pray for their daily bread, they expect God to answer. The answers do come. Sometimes the answers come in the form of checks from anonymous givers; sometimes the answers come in the form of jobs for the communes which have a business; but more often the answers come through the regular support of concerned Christians. High salaried Christian businessmen, Christians with moderate incomes, and church mission committees are getting behind the Jesus movement and providing the operating funds needed by the Jesus kids.

According to one of his residents, George Bogle needs a large amount of money every week to operate his communes, coffee houses, and seven-day-a-week radio ministry in Detroit and Pontiac. No one in his House of Prayer has a paying job, but the money comes in.

The Jesus kids in Lansing, Michigan, rent the Master's House from a member of the Central Methodist Church. He feels that they are doing a job that he and his church are not equipped to do, and he is glad to get behind their ministry.

The First Presbyterian Church of Berkeley often provides the food for Jesus rallies in their parking lot.

First Presbyterian Church, Flint, Michigan, purchased a former tobacco pipe shop near the church and turned it over to the kids for worship and Bible study. This ministry now involves as many as four hundred to five hundred young people each Sunday night.

The Catacombs, a Jesus night spot in Michigan, is operated by Balton Enterprises, a nonprofit organization. They have a nominal admission charge to defray the expenses for the food and entertainment — usually a rock gospel ensemble.

Nashville's 23rd Psalm is supported by a retired business executive and some of his friends from a men's prayer group in the area.

The Children of God have a 400-acre ranch in Texas and a six-story hotel building in Los Angeles which were both donated to them by an older man who is interested in their 600-member nationwide group. The Children of God themselves turn over all of their worldly goods (although few have much to turn over) to the group as part of their communal relationship.

The White Whale, used for Bible rap sessions and prayer meetings, is an old house on the property of the First Baptist Church of Beverly, Massachusetts. The kids use the building, but the church pays the bills.

Unlike the organized churches, few Jesus centers or communes are operated with the idea that they will build up and continue. "We'll stay here as long as the Lord wants us to," said a resident of one commune, "but we think it will probably be only a few more months."

Do they worry about their needs, or wonder what they will do for a house next year, or if the ministry will continue? Not at all! If one thing stops, God will start something else.

Julie Poston, wife of a 19-year-old elder at the 23rd Psalm, told a newspaper reporter: "This particular ministry house may not last a long time. It could be gone tomorrow, and I wouldn't say that all the people here will always be Christians. But the spirit behind the 23rd Psalm and all the houses like it — that will last forever."

Without the need for money or a job or any commitments, the Jesus kids can drift "as the Spirit leads," a concept that upsets their practical parents. Some Jesus kids refuse to work at all, even dropping out of college or high school to devote all of their time to street evangelism. Others who continue in school or at their jobs spend evenings and weekends on the streets or in Jesus meetings.

But almost all of the Jesus kids agree about one thing. The drive to accumulate things is not compatible with the drive to serve Jesus. They are not interested in goods or real estate; they just want enough to live on so that they can witness for Jesus.

"But how long can you go on like this?" parents ask. "What will you do when you get married and have a family to take care of?"

"If God wants me to get married and have a family, he'll take care of me."

"But you can't live like this forever!"

"I won't have to live like this forever; these are the last days. Jesus might be back before breakfast."

Some ministers, struggling to maintain church budgets and seeing the Jesus kids getting help from businessmen, get upset with the new movement. The ministers' attitude is not changed when the kids themselves are so casual about relating to the church.

"They come here to preach about the Jesus movement — and they get paid for it — but they don't come to worship," said a disgusted preacher. "They send their converts to the Pentecostal churches, while it's the mainline denominations that support them."

That is not entirely true. Richard Key, who runs two very straight communes (he discourages long hair and beards) in the San Francisco Bay area, has a syndicated radio program, operates a fleet of cars, and is supported by Pentecostal churches.

But many leaders of the Jesus kids admit that they do get support from the Methodists and Presbyterians. And, although they won't tell kids not to attend these supporting churches, most do not attend themselves, and they do not encourage their followers to attend. The Jesus kids get most of their Christian training from each other.

"What's wrong with us?" the church people ask. "They believe the same doctrines as we do, they don't seem to be angry at anybody, they take church money to underwrite their programs — but they won't come to church. This movement is spreading, but the church is losing even the few kids it had. What's wrong?"

"Simple," say the Jesus kids. "In the church, there isn't any body movement."

7

The Church—
No Body Movement!

A pastor is amazed!

The Jesus movement is spreading in Massachusetts.

"How can it happen here?" he asks as he watches young people crowding into the Charisma coffee house in Worcester. His feeling is common among church leaders who are seeing a revival among the young while their own churches, including their youth programs, are dying.

"If they want to meet together or worship, why don't they come to church?"

The Jesus kids are pretty much in agreement about the church. "We are not against the organized church; we just don't have time for it." Although some of the kids in the coffee houses and storefront centers do go to church, for most of the Jesus kids on the street the church does not offer what they want.

According to the Jesus kids, the church has gone so far away from real Christianity that it is now only an imitation of the faith practiced and taught by the disciples. They see the church propagating an artificial Christianity with sinful self-centered fellow travelers who want to hear the nice teachings about Jesus but refuse to follow him on the basis of the total life commitment that he requires.

"The church has had the gospel for years and hasn't done anything with it," according to a California spokesman for the Jesus kids.

"The best thing that could happen to the church," he added, "is for people to get out of it. Then those in leadership would see that something is happening on the streets."

"Free All Spiritual Prisoners" is the caption over a full-page picture of a cathedral in *Right On*. It describes what many Jesus kids feel, that church people are bound up, entrapped by their structure, and need to be liberated so that they can serve the Lord.

Arthur Blessitt has expressed the opinion that churches, which are now open only a few hours a week, should be keeping bar hours with ministers working in three shifts.

Clergymen do not react kindly to the Jesus people who dismiss them and their work so lightly. One minister wrote to the *Hollywood Free Paper:*

"I'm a pastor (over 30) out of touch with modern youth. I'm glad to support you because you are reaching people I cannot. I have one request: I don't cut you and modern youth; I wish you wouldn't cut the professional clergy and the institutional church. Some of us are really trying and are reaching people you can't, just as you reach some we can't. If we are really one body in Jesus, we help each other, O.K.?"

The Jesus kids ask, "If the organized church is supposed to be the body of Christ, and if the church is alive, why isn't there more body movement?" The "body of Christ" that the kids describe sit in padded pews, face in one direction so they can't look into each others' faces, stand when they are told to stand, sit when they are told to sit, sing and pray when they are told to sing and pray, and are entertained by a group of singers and a man, who "had better do better this week than he did last." There is no spontaneity, no joy, no expression in their actions or worship which would indicate that God has done anything in their lives worth getting excited about. Instead of praising God out of the overflowing experience of having walked with him and enjoyed him all week long, they sit in the pews to have someone do something to them. It's like going to a play or to the movies.

The church people that the Jesus kids describe have no contact with each other except for one hour a week, are usually aloof, and show little warmth to anyone visiting (unless he is a high salaried professional man. Then they flock around and say, "We could really *use* you!").

The church people rarely pray for each other; they say prayers. They would not dare reveal their own spiritual struggles to one another ("They would talk about me behind my back and question my lack of faith"), and they pay a clergyman to be the "professional Christian" while they keep reminding him that they are "Christian laymen." They claim to know Jesus, but they won't tell their neighbor about Jesus. "If you really have received 'Good News,'" the kids ask, "why do you keep it a secret?"

"They go to church meetings," a young Christian exclaimed, "but you don't *go* to church — you *are* the church if you know Jesus Christ."

A nineteen-year-old former church member wrote in a Jesus newspaper:

"I really believed that all I had to do to be a Christian was to join the church, follow the commandments (but not too closely, or else I'd be a fanatic!), give money to the church. . . . On these standards I must have been a better Christian than even St. Paul! But, if I was such a great Christian, then why was I so unhappy?"

Young people's meetings in the church are run for bored kids by adults who are usually trying to find some new gimmick to excite them enough to keep them coming to the church. Yet, down the street, Jesus kids who have left the church are crowding into Bible studies and worship meetings where they may sit for as long as three or four hours, listening to Bible messages, singing, praying, and then they go out to find their friends and tell them about Jesus.

Across the nation, explained the adult manager of a teen coffee house, it is becoming very evident that Jesus Christ does answer the needs of young people. They are finding life in Jesus centers and communes that even their church-going parents recognize as dynamic.

Calvary Chapel, pastored by forty-three-year-old "Chuck" Smith, is located on California's Santa Ana, Costa Mesa boundary. It offers an example of the kind of dynamic Christian encounter that kids are looking for. The description in *For Real* would make most pastors envious. The Wednesday night meeting (they have Bible classes every night of the week) started at seven o'clock. "Some friends and I pulled up about ten of seven. We were in for the surprise of our lives. . . ! There was standing room only outside — a thousand or more people jammed together in the chill ocean air, shoulder to shoulder. The chapel (which seats 1,000) was completely encircled with people sitting and standing both inside and out."

"Kids draw kids — it's as simple as that," say disgruntled church youth advisers. "If we had a crowd of kids in our church, we would have no trouble drawing an even larger crowd."

But, as simple as this explanation seems to be, it leaves doubts for some youth leaders.

"We had a youth retreat," explained one adult adviser, "and along with our regular church kids, we had five hippie-type young people who called themselves 'Jesus Freaks.' The church kids kept trying to find ways to avoid the Bible sessions. Their leaders had to keep going back to the cabins to rout them out. During their free time they had card games going all over the dining room. But the scene with the Jesus Freaks was entirely different. They were waiting when the Bible sessions started, asked questions, took notes, and checked out references in their Bibles. During the free time they asked the retreat leader if they could ask him some more questions about what he was teaching. The contrast was so sharp, that I find I have to rethink all the pat explanations I've heard about the Jesus kids."

An American Baptist woman in California said, "That God chose to begin his new work primarily among the hippies is no surprise. Historically God's work has been done among the dispossessed and the searching. The hippies are also, it seems, most open to the saving work of God. They are willing for him to work in their lives and in any way he sees fit. Institutionalized Christians have had a tendency to say: 'Move me, Lord, as long as you don't do this or that.' "

Feelings about the organized church differ among the various Jesus kids, but the feelings are particularly strong among the leaders of the more rigid communes.

"The institution" is the way one elder describes the church. He is quite candid about his feelings. To him, the institution is a man-run organization that has nothing to do with Christianity.

"You can't follow Jesus and still remain a part of the institution," he insists. He had been a nominal Roman Catholic, but wants no part of his former church. Even when he led his parents to a personal experience with Jesus Christ, he did not encourage them to go back to the church for teaching. They just stay home and teach themselves.

"If God wants them in the 'institution,' he'll tell them," he said.

"But isn't a Jesus commune sort of like a church?"

"Oh no! It's biblical."

"But didn't most churches and denominations get started because people pulled out of the established churches in order to start something that was 'more biblical' and obedient to Jesus? And didn't those same groups soon begin to establish organizational structures and forms of worship that in a few years became formalized almost like the church they left?"

But it does no good to ask those questions — the elder doesn't hear them.

"We follow Jesus," he says. The idea is inconceivable to him and other Jesus kids that they might be repeating denominational history. They seem to have a blind spot. Their group is going to be "truly Christian." But then the same attitude was probably true of the founders of present-day denominations. They probably would never have believed that they would someday have a structure something like the church organization that they broke away from.

There is already some structural evidence that Teen Challenge and The Children of God are shaping up to become a type of denomination.

Even the church ordinances or sacraments, once thought to belong to the church as an institution, are considered by the Jesus kids to belong to every member of the body of Christ.

Baptism, always by immersion, is held in lakes, the ocean, swimming pools (Pat Boone has baptized more than two hundred people in his Beverly Hills swimming pool including an entire rock band), and even the Reflecting Pool near the Lincoln Memorial in Washington, D.C.

Communion is shared informally, usually with crackers and grape juice or wine in a common cup. While the kids sit quietly praying, either in chairs or on the floor, one brother will pray and then pass the elements to the person seated closest to him.

Often as the plate or cup is passed, the person passing it will explain to the person receiving it from him, "This represents the body of Christ broken for you, Bill"; or "John, Jesus loves you. He shed his blood on the cross for you." Singing resumes after Communion, with deep emotion. People will lift their hands in praise and adoration, and prayers begin to come from all parts of the room, many in unknown tongues.

Sophisticated church people are surprised by the Jesus kids' literal interpretation of Scripture. They believe that the entire Bible is the inspired Word of God. The Ten Commandments and the Sermon on the Mount are to be followed without compromise. Satan is very real, and hell is certain for any who do not accept Jesus Christ as their personal Savior. They preach strongly against the sins of the world — drugs, alcohol, promiscuity, pride, and laziness. The great commission, given by Jesus to go into all the world to preach the gospel, means for the Jesus kids the world where they are — the street.

When church people see what the Jesus kids are doing on the street and decide that they too should be more actively involved in witnessing, the results are sometimes more negative than positive. When church people try to witness about Jesus Christ, they usually prove what the street kids have been saying about them all along, that they have been caught up in programs and church structures for so long that they don't know how to be responsive as human beings to other people. Not knowing how to communicate real feelings to other people, and being a "preached at" group, they continue to throw out words at people and they communicate frozen hostility even when they sincerely want to witness. People accustomed to living behind walls learn Scripture verses and church words to throw over their walls, but they don't come out from behind their walls because they need those defenses. The result is that while these evangelists ask, "Won't you accept Jesus?" nonverbally what the kids hear is, "I would like to bring you to Jesus, but I don't really want to bring you to me." Or some even communicate, "Jesus loves you and wants you, but I don't."

When the same people decide that they really ought to do something about "those hippies," the result is even worse. On the one hand, they would like to bring "those people" to Christ, but that feeling is countered by shock and disdain for the way that the street people dress and act. If guilt, or the feeling that they should overcome their natural inclinations, does send them out on the streets, the barriers are usually so high that they end up communicating their own dislike rather than a seeking, loving Savior.

One Sunday afternoon in Berkeley's Sproul Plaza, three different church groups gathered within one hundred feet of each other to witness to the hippies.

On one side, dressed in suits and ties and looking like people of 1950 dropped into a 1970's scene, a church group huddled tightly together for protection while their speaker ventured out a couple of feet in front to preach to the crowd through a loudspeaker. He, and the people who later give testimonies, talked at the kids, saying things that really did not relate to the kids where they were. Every "witness" ignored the questions shouted to him from the crowd and talked rapidly to get his speech finished so that he could retreat back into the huddle. No one left the protection of the group to talk to the kids individually. When they had finished talking and had sung a few songs, they packed up their loudspeaker and left.

Opposite them, a preacher from a different group was shouting as loudly as he could about the love of God. Hippies in front of him shouted questions, but he ignored them, raising his voice above theirs. One kid kept yelling, "I'm trying to ask you a question. Listen to me! Listen to me!"

But the preacher kept on repeating louder and louder, "If you will read the Word of God, if you will read the Word of God — "

"Listen to me!"

"If you will read the Word of God — " a milk carton hit him on the shoulder, thrown by a girl who was disgusted that he wasn't listening, but he ignored that too.

A middle-aged man in the crowd shouted, "Why don't you listen to his question? You guys don't even read your own Bibles. Jesus taught the people around him. Jesus taught that you should love your neighbor. I don't see any of that love in you people."

In an angry, frantic effort to get his point across, the preacher began again, shouting, "If you will read the word of God — "

Seated by the preacher's feet, oblivious to all the shouting, a hippie was strumming his guitar and singing while another guy stood directly in front of the preacher fondling his braless open-bloused girl friend.

Between the frightened church group on one side and the angry preacher on the other, another church group had erected a cartoon board describing the plan of salvation using comic book characters. Apparently this was an attempt at communication that could not be interrupted with questions.

The next day the Jesus kids were in the same place. Some passed out tracts, a few sat near a book table or on the ground, but nobody was preaching at the kids. They quietly talked to the kids one to one, taking plenty of time to listen to their questions and answering them so that they understood. Instead of just repeating a "plan of salvation" they listened to the thoughts about God being expressed by the other person, and then opened their Bibles to passages that would help to bring understanding. They worked calmly, with that "you-are-an-important-person" attitude that is so characteristic of the Jesus kids. They were obviously not trying to "witness to those people"; they were sharing a wonderful gift with a new-found friend.

The contrast between the church people on Sunday and the Jesus kids on Monday shows why the Jesus kids are winning people to Jesus Christ. It also shows why they really have their doubts about the reality of faith in church people. The kids feel that people who are secure in their faith and know what they believe are not afraid to listen to people and relate to them on a personal level. The person who is unsure of what he believes and is too frightened to be warmly human may only have slogans about Jesus, not a personal experience with him.

Their security in Christ enables the Jesus kids to relax in their witnessing. A student at Vanderbilt University said, "I thought they [the Jesus kids] would be rather simple-minded, arrogant, probably have this loud, triumphant attitude, saying 'everybody else is wrong' — Well, they weren't like that at all."

The same inability to be responsive to non-Christians also blocks many church people from being responsive to the Jesus kids as fellow Christians, because "they are so different from us."

The Jesus kids are a part of their youth culture just as the adults are a part of their culture; neither culture comes from the New Testament. Yet many church people who are willing to accept the Jesus kids qualify that acceptance by adding, "if they wear ties, shave, and get a haircut." Their attitude is "If they are really Christians, why don't they look like Christians?"

Even churches that are willing to overlook "their strange clothes" want to pour the kids into their church mold regarding forms of worship. Prayers are great if they are general ("God bless everybody and the missionaries abroad, Amen!"), but not acceptable if they are personal, or bluntly honest, or even charismatic. Adults are shocked by kids who break away from the printed bulletin and respond to God out of the fullness of what is inside of them. There is no fellowship when one group is uptight about the other group, and the Jesus kids know it.

Other churches respond to the kids by offering them something that is "what the young people like." Only the church people do not know usually what the young people like because they have not been listening to them. So they create programs that have more emphasis on method than content. They offer all kinds of innovative programs that do not teach anything.

Still others, feeling that the kids must be forced to look at more than salvation, lean toward social issues, political problems, and current events. Although they don't suggest, as does the editor of the *Los Angeles Free Press*, that the Jesus kids are cop-outs in the battle for revolution, they feel that they have ignored some of the crucial issues of the day.

The Jesus kids are looking for the kind of Christian fellowship that offers both an orthodoxy in doctrine and an orthodoxy in life-style.

If they go to a fundamental, evangelical, Bible-preaching church, they find people who have assumed that being Christian means doing things their way. They have accepted Christ into their hearts and souls, but their lives are not particularly Christian. The Jesus kids see in these churches people who cannot distinguish between the teachings of the Bible and the teachings of their own culture. So instead of meeting people who have been transformed by the renewing of their minds, they find people who cannot give up the control of their culture, the lust for things, the drive for social status, and the racial hatreds. They find people who quote the New Testament but have not adopted the New Testament life-style with its different set of goals.

On the other hand, when they find a church group that talks about practicing the Christian life-style and puts emphasis on love in the Christian community, they usually find that such a church does not know how to bring people into the Christian community. They cannot, or will not, point people to a personal acceptance of Jesus Christ as Savior and Lord.

Therefore, since the Jesus kids have trouble finding people who are orthodox in doctrine and life-style, they avoid the church. They say of the church:

"It is man's institution."

"The church is stagnant."

"There is no body movement."

"Do you know what I would like to see?" asked one of the Jesus kids. "I'd like to see the church people throw away their printed bulletins, worship on some day other than Sunday, have someone other than a clergyman lead, and allow God to do what he has always wanted to do."

If the church has problems, the New Testament epistles and church history indicate that it always has had them. By avoiding the church, the kids have also cut themselves off from the teachings of older, wiser saints who have experienced many years of struggling with church problems and trying to live for Jesus.

Because it spurns the help of these older Christians, many people are looking at the Jesus movement and asking, "Will it last?"

8

Will It Last?

"Isn't this Jesus movement just another fad?"

For his answer, a Jesus kid turned the pages in his Bible to a passage and read: "And now I say unto you, Refrain from these men and let them alone: for if this counsel or this work be of men, it will come to nought: But if it be of God, ye cannot overthrow it; lest haply ye be found even to fight against God" (Acts 5:38-39, KJV).

"If this is a fad," he said, "it has been going on for nearly two thousand years."

Writing in the *Hollywood Free Paper,* a young man expressed the feeling of many Jesus kids: "Please pray that Jesus will not become just another fad to some people, but that people will really know Jesus as their Savior, liberator, and friend. After all, Jesus is the Only Way, and anything short of trusting in Him just won't make it."

The majority of Jesus kids do not want Jesus to be just another trip. Although there are some kids who go running around the streets and beaches "leading people to Christ" only to leave them and run on to the next prospect, most Jesus kids are concerned about the spiritual growth of their new brothers and sisters. They explain carefully what it means to belong to Christ; they work the new ones into a Bible study where they can learn discipleship and watch them to see if their decision for Christ is genuine or just words. The Jesus kids are zealous, but most of them are also concerned that people really do meet Jesus, not just learn words about Jesus. Their experience with the church has taught them the danger of easy Christianity.

A former Jesuit priest and Catholic magazine editor, who is now married and teaching at Emory University, thinks the Jesus movement is real. He likened the enthusiasm and dedication of the Jesus kids to the feelings of a novitiate training in Roman Catholic orders. Most observers of the Jesus kids agree that what they see happening is a real spiritual fire that is spreading and encompassing both hippies and straight kids.

There are kids who turn to the Jesus movement because it seems to be the latest thing to do. Dr. Hudson T. Armerding told one thousand people at the twenty-ninth annual Convention of the National Association of Evangelicals that there was a danger of faddism based on an incomplete view of the person and work of Christ. He warned that people could be superficially attracted to this kind of thing because it is exciting.

Parents know that teenagers will quickly pick up the latest fad and use the latest words whether they are slang words or words about Jesus. There will always be young people who follow along, not really knowing what it is that they are doing.

Commercial interests capitalize on any movement that promises a good money market, and the Jesus movement is no exception. So-called Jesus music will play over and over again on the radio until the kids are saturated with a watered-down version of Jesus Christ, and then they will go on to something else.

There will be adults who see only the fad aspects of the Jesus movement and decide that it is all a fad. They will point to some youth whose actions prove that the adults are right. Parents whose teenagers have claimed Jesus Christ as their Savior may not really know if it is real or not until after the craze ends. They will be watching their children, knowing that it takes more than a Jesus sweatshirt and a few Jesus records to make a lifelong disciple. The Jesus kids know this, too, and are praying for some real conversions in spite of the Jesus records and Jesus paraphernalia that are capturing some of the youth and innoculating them against a real experience with Jesus Christ.

Pat Boone, who was asked to leave the Church of Christ because of his experience with speaking in tongues, said in a newspaper interview: "I think the Jesus movement is real and legitimate. It may be a shallow experiment for many, sort of an in thing to do. . . . Personally, I know it is a great deal more than that. . . ."

The movement is a great deal more than that to the people who have studied their Bibles and memorized Scripture so that they can be faithful followers of Jesus Christ and can answer the questions of other seeking young people. It is not a fad to those who have attended the Jesus training centers or to those who have gone on to Bible schools and theological seminaries. A fad could not cause people to long prayerfully for someone to meet Jesus and then produce the joy that comes when that person accepts Jesus. People caught up in the bandwagon aspects of a fad do not go that far or experience that much.

The Jesus kids say that the movement is going to last until Jesus comes, and they add, "It won't be long now." They point to Acts 2:17, the most quoted passage of Scripture among the Jesus kids, as proof that God is winding things up in their day:

"And it shall come to pass in the last days, saith God, I will pour out of my Spirit upon all flesh: and your sons and your daughters shall prophesy, and your young men shall see visions, and your old men shall dream dreams" (KJV).

"God is doing that now," they excitedly announce. They are firmly convinced that they are the people in whom God's prophecy is being fulfilled. They are the forerunners of the second coming of Jesus.

"How can this be a fad," they ask, "when it was predicted in the Bible? A fad is something that people start."

The Jesus kids see other signs that point to the second coming:

The European Common Market — the world's last and most powerful dictator will control this ten-nation confederacy. He in turn will be controlled by Satan.

The increase in wars — there have been forty-four wars since World War II; twelve of them were major wars.

Thermonuclear warfare — the Jesus kids see this as the intense heat referred to in 2 Peter 3:10-12.

Religionless Christianity — they see it around them now.

All of these signs convince the Jesus kids that Jesus is coming back very soon. Their job is to see to it that people hear the gospel before Jesus comes. When he comes, the rapture will be — as they describe it — "the ultimate trip."

For the Jesus kids, Jesus is the message. He is coming too soon to talk of anything else. Although some of the kids will occasionally speak of war, ecology, or women's "lib," most of the

Jesus people ignore social issues except as a take-off point for witnessing. War, hatred, even poverty, come as part of man's inhumanity to his fellowman, which is sin.

What about changing political structures, human rights, or improving the local school board? They believe that Jesus Christ in the hearts of men will change the world. Social ills call for repentance, "You must be born again." Man must be turned around; he must surrender himself to Jesus.

At several turning points in history, there has been renewal in the church with a "turning-around emphasis" that brought change to the people who follow Jesus. Such a change happened in the Reformation. At the time that the Reformation began, no one could have imagined its long-range effects. When the Wesley revivals swept America and Great Britain, some people laughed and called it "the silly work of those Methodists." But no one today can deny the effect of those revivals on the Christian church. People with a sense of church history hesitate to apply the word "fad" to anything with the scope and magnitude that marks the Jesus movement.

Few who attend Bible studies or prayer meetings conducted by the Jesus kids doubt that the movement, in some form or other, will last. The question of longevity is usually raised by those who have never attended. To see a room jammed full of young people studying the Bible for two or three hours at a time and to hear them asking questions (about the Godhead and church history and theology) that are rarely asked in adult church school classes convince most people that the information they learn and the desire to know the Bible will always be a part of these kids, long after they are mature adults. And if they outgrow the types of meetings that they have now and go back to the church, they will take their new information and their new study habits with them.

Even if the Jesus movement is a fad and does not last, it will have lasting effects. Theologian Martin Marty commented that five years from now we may have some better Presbyterians because they were part of this movement.

As the movement spreads, the churches are going to gain, if only from the side effects. A Baptist deacon, who opens his home to the Jesus kids for Bible study and worship, told them that they ought to be tithing to their church. They listened, examined the Bible references that he showed them on tithing, and agreed. Whether they remain in the church or not, tithing will be a part of them and their Bible teaching. It will influence their parents and the kids they introduce to Christ. The work of the Christian church will benefit for years to come.

A girl asked her Bible study group for help because she could not control her cutting tongue. The others in the room showed real concern and promised to help her. They also pointed out in the Scriptures how God could help her with her sharp tongue. Any pastor would welcome that girl into his congregation. She would not be afraid to admit her problems, she would show other reserved Christians that it is not embarrassing to admit shortcomings, and she would create a fellowship of the concerned where people would help one another to become the people God wants them to be. No one could play word games or be artificial around her. She would reach out in love to others and expect others to reach out in love to her.

Young people who came out of churches where they were only spectator Christians are now involved zealously in the ministry of healing and preaching. They are, in fact, what the church was originally designed to be. They will never be the same again, nor will the church people they meet be the same. They have what so many church people have lacked and wanted but, until now, have not been able to identify.

The Jesus kids are teaching that they are God's people and that there are no such things as "laymen" among the people of God. They know that there are many gifts, and some are teachers, some pastors, some administrators, and the like, but they also know that all are chosen by God for discipleship. Trusting Jesus Christ as Savior and Lord is not just mental assent to him. It is a commitment of their lives, which means they belong to him with all their heart, soul, mind, and strength. It is an active, serving commitment. They state categorically that they will never go back to the comfortable pew as spectators. Belonging to Jesus Christ means too much to them. They have been changed, and they insist on practicing that changed life.

"Well, what about the backsliders?" asks a middle-aged woman. "There have to be backsliders in a movement like this."

"There are," a girl admitted. "Many who come to Jesus because they are looking for an escape, or an easy answer to life's problems, or because their friends seem to be excited about their new faith, drop away. But," she quickly added, "look at the thousands who go on with Jesus!"

Wesley Smith, who leads Bible studies for the Jesus kids in Michigan, has seen a lot of young people come to Christ and then slip back into their old ways.

"But," he said, "that isn't always a bad thing."

He explained that these youth reach a low point, as every Christian does, because the Christian life is not always a happy "mountaintop experience." They have doubts; they question whether their faith is real or just an emotional experience; and if the pressures of life build up, they may even go back on drugs or to their old ways.

But, having met Jesus, the old thrills do not compare. The emptiness of the old life really comes through when they contrast it to the basic, deeply rooted peace that they have in Jesus. After these low points, they come back to Christ; and they come back even stronger in their faith than they were before, because they have compared living the old life with living in Christ. Jesus has proved to them that a life with him, with all of its ups and downs, is far more meaningful and rewarding than the life they once had.

"The Jesus movement is a fad," said a pastor. "The shallowness and quackery of it ought to be exposed."

"Maybe the church as we have known it is the fad," retorted a Jesus kid. "Maybe the shallowness and quackery of it are now being exposed, and people are beginning to see in this spiritual revolution that Jesus Christ is alive."

There will always be some people who get on any bandwagon that passes by. This tendency is particularly true of youth, especially if the fad is sensational. For such persons, the Jesus movement will only be a passing fad, and any "decision" they make will probably be forgotten. That cannot be prevented. The sad part is that they will probably go around saying, "Oh yes, I tried Jesus. Now I think that it's only emotionalism."

For most, however, the movement is real, and the spiritual result in their own lives is proof enough. Whether they are street kids or "at home" church kids, the Jesus revolution with its evangelism, Bible studies, and creative worship will remain a part of them.

But there is a danger in what is happening in the Jesus movement. The danger is not that the Jesus movement will be a passing fad. The danger comes in the overwhelming concern of the kids that it *not* be a fad.

Most of the Jesus kids are so genuinely committed to Jesus Christ and want so much to be totally dedicated followers that they grab onto any teaching that appears to offer them more biblical content. Their eagerness to learn and grow in the Christian faith has made them vulnerable to any authoritative teacher who comes along.

Most of the Jesus kids, through prayer and good teachers, are growing strong in the Christian faith. There are others, however, who are starting to ride around in many different directions on some very strange theological hobbyhorses. And they label what they do a "Holy Spirit function."

9

Holy Spirit Function

The Jesus kids call what they do a response to "the leading of the Holy Spirit." And for many of them this is a sincere explanation.

The ministry of the Holy Spirit in their lives, teaching, comforting, guiding, is very obvious to an observer. There is a relaxed trust in the Spirit that is refreshing to the busy, fussing, average Christian who is "trying to do the work of the Lord" and is exhausted in the trying.

Go with a group of Jesus kids in Glendale, California, as they witness to shoppers on the streets. While the girls of the house cook the evening meal, and some of the men of the commune prepare for an evening meeting in another part of the city, several of the brothers pick up copies of a little red booklet entitled *Personal Bible Verses — Comfort, Assurance, Salvation* and start walking toward one of the main streets.

Before they get to their destination, they stop, put their arms around each other as if they were forming a football huddle, and pray that God will bless their efforts and lead them to people who will respond to Jesus. They are not embarrassed to be praying on the street with pedestrians looking at them; they are confident that the Lord is there.

With booklets in hand and Bibles ready, they begin by approaching the first person they see. An observer who may be a little shy at first has to be impressed by the sincerity and warmth of these men and by the quiet "Lord Jesus, you show us who we should talk to," prayer whispered as they walk along the street.

They are very polite.

"May we share with you a word about Jesus?"

"Would you like a booklet that gives some promises from the Bible?"

They approach the elderly, the young, and the middle-aged alike. However, the response to them from each of the age groups is very different. The young listen carefully and even ask questions. They are very responsive. The elderly listen too and are not offended by the long hair, beards, and hippie clothes of these young Christians. But the middle-aged people with panic in their voices say, "No, thank you," and move over to the curb to avoid contact. A man and woman sitting in a parked car roll up their windows and lock their doors.

A Christian brother from another Jesus house comes around the corner across the street. They see each other and immediately point their index fingers to the sky in the "Jesus is the One Way" sign, and shout across the busy intersection, "Praise the Lord!"

The booklets are quickly given away, so the men start back to the house for supper, feeling that they were led by the Holy Spirit to the people that they talked to about Jesus. They have a good feeling that maybe God has been working in the life of that man or that boy and they were one link in a chain of unfolding events in those lives which would cause them to respond to Jesus Christ. Who can say? they muse; maybe it was the right time for some of those people to be confronted with the need to accept Jesus.

They help one another, discussing what they did and said. They are eager to learn. If an older Christian is with them, especially if he has had more witnessing experience, they will question him:

"How do you present Christ to someone on the street?"

"What's the best way to approach a person who . . . ?"

"How would you have answered the man who said . . . ?"

Most of them are new Christians themselves. They have had very little Christian instruction, so they are hungry for teaching about the Bible or witnessing or any aspect of the Christian life. As a result, they will accept anybody as a teacher if he gives evidence of being a brother in Christ.

This eagerness to learn leads some young Christians into

trouble. The person who appears to be a good teacher may be pushing his own theological bias. The zeal to learn, which is so characteristic of the young Christians, is not always balanced by the wisdom and discernment needed to distinguish between the various teachings that they get.

"We had a tremendous Christian commune going here," said a pastor in Albuquerque, "until some other Jesus kids came along who had some different Bible verses and convinced these kids that they ought to pack up and follow them. Now the house that had such a good witnessing ministry to the transient youth is empty."

In a Southern Illinois community, a twenty-three-year-old girl operates a leather working shop and uses it as an opportunity to witness to her customers. She is a very happy, vivacious girl, who finds it a joy to do her leather work for Jesus. But she confessed that she had cried many nights over the teaching of a Jesus group whose members insisted that she was sold out to the devil because she worked for money.

She believed that as a Christian she should not be in debt to anyone, and the leather shop was paying off her bills.

"How can I tell somebody about Jesus if I owe him money?" she asked.

She admitted that it took many nights of praying and a lot of emotional struggle before she could come to peace about her job.

A similar group from Missoula, Montana, travels around the country "witnessing for Jesus" and telling anyone who has a job that he is lost.

"We trust the Lord," they say. "Anyone who works is grubbing for the dollar. He worships a house and a Cadillac. Because his heart is set on those things, he isn't sold out to Jesus."

If another Christian tries to show that he does not worship the dollar or things but only works to support his family, he is told that he has not given up everything for Jesus.

"But God led me to my job," a Christian argues. "I prayed about it, and this is what God wants me to do. Besides, by working I can earn money to support the Lord's work."

"It isn't the Lord's work," is their response. "The person who has a job is not of God; he is of Satan."

These "Children of God," as they call themselves, refuse to

listen to Scriptures which indicate that Peter fished, Paul made tents, and Luke practiced medicine. Also they will not admit that when they travel around the country on their witnessing missions and stop at Christian homes for a meal or to sleep, those people are able to provide for them only because they have jobs.

No matter how hard a person tries to show this group that they could not exist if there were not working people to provide for them, they will not listen. What seems to anybody else to be a logical argument is completely ignored by them. They won't even respond. They just go right on repeating, "You've got to be sold out to Jesus. If you have a job, you serve your job; you do not serve Jesus."

This group is becoming a closed sect operating on an idea that allows them to accept the support of working people (they were given a hotel for their headquarters), but it does not allow them to admit that the people who support them may be Christians. They want to be like the apostle Paul and be free to go on missionary journeys, but they ignore the fact that Paul acknowledged the support he received from other Christians.

The leaders of this group have given their followers an emotion-laden belief ("You've got to be sold out to Jesus") which sounds good to many young Christians because they don't want anything to stand in the way of a total commitment to Christ. Sincere Jesus kids are often captured by this kind of teaching.

The guilt which will overwhelm them when they find that they do have to work to eat, or when they admit that they are being supported by Christians who do work, could cause some deep psychological problems. If they do not hear some balanced Christian teaching about work and loyalty to Christ, they will feel like backsliders who no longer trust the Lord. Some may even become convinced that they belong to Satan. Those who think it through and reject the teaching may go all the way and reject everything else that they were taught about Jesus.

Many Jesus kids are ripe for this teaching about work because they have already decided that nothing must stand between them and total discipleship. Many do not have jobs, not because work is bad in itself, but because a job takes too much time and they want to give all of their time to sharing Jesus Christ with people on the streets. Thus, they have a positive reason for not working. So when the "Children of God" people come along, they have a ready-made audience for their beliefs, particularly if the beliefs which they present appear to be very biblical.

This group also has a ready-made audience when they approach the Jesus kids with another belief, "The church is unbiblical. It isn't of God."

Many Jesus kids have had all they want of the church. They are convinced that they are better off without it because church people seem to be content with a comfortable Jesus, ignore the call to commitment, and rarely witness to people about the saving power of Christ. But this attitude toward the church is not a dogma as much as it is a feeling of "why waste time with an institution that isn't doing anything for Jesus." With the "Children of God," however, it *is* a dogma. They teach that the church is unbiblical; it is not of God. An attempt to reason with them ends up in a disjointed argument that goes something like this:

"The church is unbiblical, it isn't of God."

"But the church is the body of Christ. If you are a Christian as you say you are, you are part of the church."

"No, we come together and share all things commonly."

"But that's the church. That's what it is to be part of the people of God. The church does share commonly."

"Revelation 17 says that the Roman Catholic Church is the whore of Babylon. You're of the whore."

"I don't see where Revelation says that; but anyway, I'm not a Roman Catholic."

"But you are part of her offspring."

"Do you mean any person who is related to any church body is part of the 'whore' in the book of Revelation?"

"They are all man's organization. They are all of the whore; and to follow Jesus, you've got to leave the whore."

The same mind-set controls a group that believes that the King James Version of the Bible is the only true and literal Word of God. If someone is reading a different version, they will quote:

> For I testify unto every man that heareth the words of the prophecy of this book, If any man shall add unto these things, God shall add unto him the plagues that are written in this book:
> And if any man shall take away from the words of the book of this

prophecy, God shall take away his part out of the book of life, and out of the holy city, and from the things which are written in this book (Revelation 22:18-19 KJV).

When it is explained that these verses also appear in the Revised Standard Version, Today's English Version, and other versions, they refuse to listen. "The King James Version alone is the inspired Word of God," they insist.

One exasperated person retorted: "What about the original Greek? Why don't you go back and read that? Why bother with any translation?"

"We don't know anything about that," came the reply. "This is God's translation; this alone is his Word." And they went on to explain that since the King James Version is the Word of God, people who read anything else are not reading the Word of God. So, it follows, they are not really Christians.

On the streets of Hollywood, the young witnesses of the "Christian Foundation" give more evidence of what can happen when strong leaders get hold of young people and teach them their beliefs. The husband-and-wife team who lead the group of about three hundred young people send them out on the streets night and day to pass out literature about their group in the hope that they will recruit more young people, who in turn can be sent out on the streets to recruit, and so on. It is a program built on fear.

"We fear the Lord."

"Wonderful," says the Christian to whom they are talking, "so do I." But he quickly learns that they mean a different kind of fear.

"Just as a child is afraid of a father who will beat him if he doesn't behave, we must fear God because his judgment could come down on us at any time."

They are convinced that there can be no security simply by trusting in the saving work of Christ. They must continually prove to God that they are faithful to him by going out on the streets with their mimeographed invitations to their group meetings. They work to keep God happy, but they never seem to know when they have done enough to please him.

Even though they call themselves Christians and tell people that Jesus died for their sins, they seem unable to distinguish between believing in Jesus and attendance at their meetings.

Their words are about Jesus, but their literature is about their group. There is no evidence that they know what they are saying when they talk about Jesus. Their "witnessing" is not an attempt to win people to the Savior but to simply throw out words about Jesus to as many people as they can. They want to reach numbers. Every pedestrian on Hollywood Boulevard between Vine and Grauman's Chinese Theatre is approached. Teams of girls are out during the day, and teams of boys are out at night.

If a team meets a Christian on the street, the encounter is both comical and sad. Ten feet in front of their approaching "prospect" they shout out:

"Jesus died for you."

The Christian responds, "I know."

They ignore the reply. Still walking fast, they come up to him and say, "And He is coming again."

"I believe that, too," says the Christian.

But still not hearing, and now already ten feet past their "prospect," they shout back over their shoulders, "And Jesus will save your soul from hell." Then they are gone.

A hippie described his encounter with someone like that:

"This Jesus kid was talking at me, real loud and peppy, like he was hopped up or something. I kept trying to stop him so that I could ask a question about Jesus, but he kept quoting one Bible verse after another. Since I was a little bit high on LSD, I began to wonder if he was really there. So I asked him, 'Are you really here?' Fortunately he answered me, because I was beginning to think that I was imagining him."

On Berkeley's Telegraph Avenue, a girl with a bouquet of flowers approached a Jesus kid of this kind.

"Would you like to buy a flower?" she asked.

His reply was a sharp "You need Jesus!"

"I have Jesus," she responded politely.

"You've got to ask Him to save you."

"I have asked Jesus to save me."

"You've got to be baptized in the name of Jesus."

"I have been baptized in the name of Jesus, and I belong to the fellowship of 'The Way.' "

"Oh, well then, you are not a Christian."

"But I am a Christian."

"No, if you belong to that group, you don't really belong to

Jesus. Besides you've got to be baptized in the Holy Spirit."

"I have received the baptism of the Holy Spirit." She kept her composure and continued to smile at him.

In frustration he started to walk off and then turned to someone else who had been talking with another one of his group and asked, "How do you baptize?"

"In the name of the Father, the Son, and the Holy Spirit," came the reply.

"You don't follow the Scriptures. The Bible says: 'Repent and be baptized everyone of you in the name of Jesus Christ for the remission of your sins.' " And he walked away.

A narrow or twisted view of Scripture can sap the strength of the Jesus movement. When people get hold of one idea and ride it hard, they can drag other well-meaning but untaught people along with them. This can create some disastrous effects.

A pastor in California had to do a lot of talking to convince a young man that he should not leave his wife. The young man had accepted Christ at a Jesus commune where the residents were teaching themselves without outside help. They told him that his wife was not a Christian and that it was unbiblical for a Christian to be married to a non-Christian. "Be ye not unequally yoked together with unbelievers: for what fellowship hath righteousness with unrighteousness? and what communion hath light with darkness?" (2 Corinthians 6:14, KJV). The wife tearfully insisted that she was a Christian, but he left her pregnant and destitute and moved into the commune.

Fortunately, the pastor was able to get them back together, but he failed with two other husbands who left their wives for the same reason.

Another teaching which is strongly emphasized to the Jesus kids is the charismatic gift of speaking in tongues. Because the charismatic teachers seem to be on fire for Christ, and non-charismatic people (particularly those in denominational churches) often do not, the kids naturally assume that the difference is in the tongues.

The young people find it easy to come to that conclusion. In many (to them) unexciting churches, there is little evidence put on the Holy Spirit in a Christian's life. In charismatic circles there is much emphasis put on the Holy Spirit. But in the charismatic circles the Holy Spirit and tongues are so tied up together that a new Christian has difficulty separating them. What comes across to him is that the Holy Spirit is evidenced in a believer's life through the speaking in tongues. Those who have tongues have the Holy Spirit; therefore, he concludes, those who have the Holy Spirit must have tongues. He sees enthusiastic Christians, who are concerned for the lost and eager to know the Bible, speaking in tongues; he compares them with unenthusiastic Christians, who do not care much about reaching the lost, do not bother with the Bible, and do not speak in tongues. The conclusion to him is obvious — one group has the Holy Spirit; the other group does not.

The Jesus kids do not realize, nor are they taught, that a person may be either spiritually alive or spiritually dead, but that his spiritual condition cannot be measured by whether or not he speaks in tongues.

For some teachers of the Jesus kids, the emphasis on speaking in tongues is as strong as the emphasis on the new birth. Five minutes after one woman accepted Christ, several people had her in another room praying for her to receive the Holy Spirit — which of course meant tongues. They prayed with her until she did begin speaking in an unknown tongue. Then they all rejoiced that she had received the Holy Spirit. There was no teaching about her new-found faith, no chance for the woman to grow as a believer or to learn the place of tongues in the Bible. She naturally wanted to belong to God in every dimension, so she did what she was told God wanted her to do.

In any Jesus people prayer meeting it is not uncommon to hear people break out into tongues. For most, the experience is genuine and meaningful and appears to be a gift of God. But when a roomful of people begin singing a song in harmony using the same "unknown" tongue as if it were written on their song sheets or insist that everyone must speak in unknown tongues if he is really Holy Spirit filled, then older Christians go back to their Bibles for another look at what is said about the gifts of the Holy Spirit.

Studies in chapters twelve through fourteen in First Corinthians are usually conducted in such a way that the Jesus kids are made to see tongues not as a gift of God (a minor gift in a list of many) but as a requirement for every believer as proof that he has the Holy Spirit. What God intended as a gift, man has made a requirement. The Holy Spirit is no longer God's spirit of power. He is neatly packaged and distributed.

But as long as the established churches give the impression that they do not even know whether there is a Holy Spirit or not, the Jesus kids will continue to turn to teachers who seem to know about him. Teachers who are poorly taught can create some real problems.

In a storefront Jesus center which is run for teenagers by adults, a fourteen-year-old boy heard people talk about Jesus and asked to receive Christ as his Savior.

Immediately he was taken into a basement room, which was dingy and dark, and all of the adults in the group put their hands on him and began praying that he receive the Holy Spirit. He was so frightened by all those people crowding around him in the dark room, many speaking in unknown tongues, that he could not respond to them at all.

When they brought him out, ashen-faced, they pushed him toward a college student who himself spoke in tongues and said, "Here, you work with him; we can't do anything with him."

Fortunately, the young man who took over was a very sensitive Christian.

"Look," he said, "you accepted Jesus Christ as your Savior; that's what is important."

He showed him verses in the Bible that give assurance to believers that they are children of God.

Then he said kindly, "Try to forget what happened just now in the basement. If God wants you to have certain gifts, he will give them. But that is something you can think about and pray about as you grow as a Christian. You go home now, tell your parents and your pastor that you accepted Christ tonight, and listen to them."

The eagerness to be taught and to be filled with the Holy Spirit has brought forth some dynamic young Christians among the Jesus kids. But that desire to learn has also opened the door for all kinds of confusion and lack of balance in doctrinal teaching.

The responsibility of the Christian church would seem to be to offer the instruction in the faith that these young new Christians so desperately need. But before the church can do so, it must first take a good long look at its image.

Anger or rebellion has not driven many of the Jesus kids away from the church, but the conviction that the people in the churches really don't want to follow Jesus has driven them away. Church games, not discipleship, seem to be the activity of the church. Young people will need some proof before they are convinced otherwise.

Even if the kids have misunderstood the church, the church cannot indignantly demand that the kids come see for themselves. If Christians in the church care about these street Christians and are concerned that they be strong men and women for Christ, then they must go to the kids. Church people who know the seeking love of God cannot self-righteously say, "Why should I go to them? Let them come and find out that we know Jesus, too." If a Christian has a need, his brother in Christ does not wait — he goes to him.

The streets are teeming with new Christians who are desperately longing for the depth of teaching that mature Christian men and women in the church can offer them. Teaching them may require a new acceptance and openness on the part of older believers and a renewed dedication to Jesus Christ that may bring about some changes in the church. But most Christians agree that no organization or structure is more important than people.

The Jesus kids believe that these are the last days, the days in which God said, "I will pour out of my spirit upon all flesh." Perhaps it is time for the church to believe that, too, and take on a new spirit.

10

A New Spirit

A Ph.D. in a university church told his pastor, "My wife and I are looking again at what God wants for our lives, and it's almost frightening. We just haven't gone far enough with him."

He is not alone. The excitement of following Jesus in a whole-hearted "no holds barred," committed way is beginning to appeal to many people in the church. Many have been nudged into it by the Jesus kids.

Christians are noticing the spiritual revival taking place in the streets and are asking, "Couldn't it happen in the church, too?"

The somewhat sterile, ordinary church functions, which once easily passed for acceptable Christianity, are now more noticeably dissatisfying when contrasted to the personal responsiveness to Jesus Christ that the Jesus kids are demonstrating. Many church people are seeing in the Jesus movement much more than teenagers off on another fad. They are sensing a joy and a commitment that they had long ago forgotten was possible, and they are beginning to want it again for themselves.

A Southern Baptist minister in the Southwest said his congregation is starting to get very serious about putting Jesus Christ first in their lives.

"Before they were content just to be Baptists," he said, "now they want to be Christians."

There is a nucleus of people, a small-group fellowship, in his church that is attempting to put into practice New Testament Christianity. And they learned it from the kids.

"It's hard," he explained, "for adults to move into a life

where the faith is being lived the way these kids are living it. These kids are genuine; they are honest."

Changes came when the kids started pushing for a vital church. They said: "If there is anything to this business of being Christian, let's get to it. Let's not play around. Either it's real or it's not."

Not long ago only the so-called "liberal" churches accepted the life-style of the young people while the "conservative" churches considered their dress and long hair sinful. But since the Jesus kids began to show that Jesus Christ is real to them and have shown that there is no Christian dress code or Christian hair style in the New Testament, the theologically conservative churches are beginning to open their doors to the kids, and the liberal churches are wondering what has happened to their young people.

The "new birth," the transformation of life by Jesus Christ, is emphasized by the kids. The churches that will teach this doctrine and be responsive and loving to the kids as human beings of value are the churches that are drawing the young people.

The Jesus kids have had the street, and the hippie culture, and the anti-establishment trip, and the social revolution teachings. They turned from these to trust in Jesus Christ as the One who can make them new creations. They want to hear the kind of Bible teaching that points to Jesus as the only way, and they want to meet Christians who love people. They won't respond to humanistic sermons, and they won't respond to hateful, narrow, bigoted church people.

A young man who dropped out of college in his second year to devote all of his time to witnessing on the streets said:

"I took this seeking kid to church with me one Sunday. The entire sermon was about the church's need for money, and how to raise money, so we got up and left."

"On another occasion," he said, "I went to a church where a woman was talking about missionary work, but she didn't say anything about Jesus. So I asked her, 'Do you have any way of presenting Jesus Christ to people in a personal way?' Instead of answering me, she got flustered and went off on a different subject."

Then he smiled and added, "But afterwards, about twenty of

the young people invited me to their youth meeting because they wanted to know more about what I was asking. I had a great time explaining to them the way of salvation."

The kids want the content of the Christian faith that the churches could offer. A young Christian, bearded and long-haired, looking uncomfortable in a dress shirt and tie, said to a Baptist gathering: "Tell them straight; tell them plain. Jesus is ready, people; Jesus is ready to work."

Two people who travel around the country helping to establish Jesus centers and communes said, "The church people need to get excited for Christ. They've got to believe that the Lord can perform miracles. The kids really need teaching!"

Francis Cook, pastor of Calvary Baptist Church in Saginaw, Michigan, went to a Jesus people's meeting. He wanted to find out what the Jesus movement is all about. Because he went to them, instead of waiting for them to come to his church, they were responsive to him. When they found out that he believed the teachings of the Bible and taught it as God's Word, they asked him to be their Bible teacher.

"We can lead them to Christ," they told him, "but we need a Bible teacher."

Cook says that in his thirty-one years in the pastorate, he has never experienced the thrill of teaching that he is experiencing now. Wherever he goes, he tells people about the Jesus kids. He has found a whole new dimension of ministry because he has made himself available to the kids. They are what every teacher dreams about, a people who want to learn. And he does not try to make them "go get a haircut."

The biggest block for many pastors and congregations to becoming the teachers that the Jesus kids need is not their doctrine. Most church people consider themselves doctrinally conservative as far as the Bible is concerned. The real problem is their attitude toward the kids' life-style. They cannot get past the long hair, beards, clothing, and also their emphasis upon human values as more important than the gross national product.

While the church people are turned off by the kids, they continue to stress their own life-style as being "Christian." They cannot see that they are victims of their culture. They have adopted the culture of their neighbors and labeled it "Christian."

Jack Sparks of the Christian World Liberation Front points out that if people would read their Bibles, they would find that the culture which has trapped most church people is not Christian at all. Church people have tied culture and Christianity so closely together that they do not distinguish one from the other anymore. What the kids are doing in being responsive to other human beings and in putting Jesus ahead of things is far more Christian than the actions of their parents who balk at sharing anything either of the gospel or of themselves.

The Jesus kids are saying to the church that if a person says he belongs to Jesus Christ, then he must live for Jesus Christ and do the work that Jesus wants done in the world. He has made a choice, he has decided to be a disciple, and his Master comes first. The same seeking-love, the same concerns, and the same attitude about the world that are characteristic of Jesus are characteristic of the disciple. His new value system in Jesus insists that it is far more important to love people and tell them about the Savior than it is to put a second coat of wax on the car. If a follower of Jesus adopts certain aspects of his culture as a part of his life-style, he does not need to pretend or insist that his choice is "Christian" and other choices are not.

The church that puts its primary emphasis on securing new drapes for the parlor or padded cushions for the pews has lost its first love. It does little good for the church people to insist that they seek those niceties as part of their Christian witness to draw more people to the church. It has long been obvious to the kids that the people who are drawn by those things have the same values and will want even more padding to draw more like-minded people. The kids are looking for the church that is like Jesus — concerned about sick or hungry lost sheep.

"I object," exclaimed a pastor. "Do you mean to tell me that I cannot enjoy cushioned pews in the church? Do I have to go down to a storefront to please those kids? Do I have to wear sandals and let my hair grow in order to be accepted? I like a suit and tie! Why do I have to be like them?"

"You don't," reply the Jesus kids. "Pad the pews, if you feel that's what Jesus wants. Wear a suit and tie if that's the style you prefer.

"*But,* don't tell us that your style is Christian and ours is not. Let's accept one another in those peripheral things, admit that one's choice of life-style is a matter of taste, not a matter of biblical teaching, and then get on with the business of following Jesus and getting out the gospel."

The kids want a church that knows Whom it serves. The kids are still part of the youth subculture, products of a society that produced the hippies, the flower children, and the emphasis on love. They will not bother with a church that is suffocating in its narrowness, no matter how much Jesus is talked about on Sunday morning. There must be a new evangelical spirit in the church and a responsiveness to people before the kids will leave what they have in the Jesus centers and communes and begin to be part of the organized church. A few churches are showing the way.

A Baptist church in Alameda, California, is having a ministry to many types of young people, not just the street kids. They have developed new forms of worship, and old and young are finding fellowship with one another that both generations have wanted for a long time.

First Presbyterian Church in Berkeley is open to all of the various ministries of the street Christians from CWLF to Inter-Varsity. They don't try to grab the young people for church membership, although some of the kids are showing an interest in being part of the church. The church is biblical in its doctrine and warm in its concern for people.

One eighty-year-old lady prays like the young people around her, not with pious phrases but with an honest expression of her feelings. Another elderly lady greets everyone who comes to the church in a warm, grandmotherly affectionate way, not fussy, not picky, just loving in the way that she relates to people.

"This is what the kids want," the pastor explained. "Don't push them about church membership. Give them content and give them warmth, and they'll come."

A Lutheran pastor in Los Angeles is highly praised by the Jesus kids because of his love and concern for them and other people. They listen to him, soaking up his teaching. They go to him for pastoral counseling. He never insists that they adopt his life-style. He just helps them grow as Christians.

Roman Catholic Pentecostals meet each Wednesday night at Notre Dame University for praise, songs, testimonies, and Scripture. A theologian at Notre Dame said that some priests, after years of study, do not have as deep a penetration of Scripture. To these Catholics who are being renewed, their worship is not a fad. They are finding the warmth of fellowship and biblical teaching that many of their churches have not been offering them.

One priest said that the Jesus trip is simply a rediscovery of the "life-giving waters that have ever been able to flow from Christ's ancient institutions." But, these men agree, this renewal is not happening in enough churches fast enough.

The Jesus kids are teaching the adults in the church. Church members are beginning to appreciate the real genuine feelings that the kids are expressing toward God and other people. They are hearing things that they have not heard before.

A new Christian, converted during a Jesus meeting, prayed in a church, "Lord, let us rock to your rhythm." The people knew that these were not just neat sounding words, nor were they the equivalent to the standard prayer meeting prayer, "Lord, help us to be better Christians." Getting in rhythm means listening and moving to the beat given by God, not some other drummer.

When parents hear the Jesus kids pray like that and then listen to their own children who grew up in the church still saying the canned prayers and giving sterile testimonies, they begin to wonder where they fell short. Slowly, more and more people are beginning to move to where the Jesus kids are in their experience. They are beginning to add this kind of praying to their new concepts of Christian life. Prayer like this is personal; it is honest. Like creative forms of worship, contemporary music, drama, and ecumenical home study groups, the street prayers are adding a new dimension to the church and moving the church toward a new vitality.

New life has to come soon. *Christians in Action,* a paper published by the Missionary and Soul Winning Fellowship of Long Beach, California, stated in April, 1971:

In our present spiritual revolution, fires of resurrection must burn in all three Christian age-groups (youth, middle-aged, and senior citizens). The present move is taking place mainly "outside the camp" and must move inside the church to set saints ablaze. . . . In order to have the breadth, depth, and altitude to move America, every age-level must be involved. The mature levels must blend with the fire of youth, who are today's trail blazers.

When the wisdom of the mature Christian blends with the zeal of the young Christians, both will benefit. Adults need the Jesus kids in the church to help it come alive. The Jesus kids need the adults to help them grow into a balanced Christian life.

If they are to relate to the youth, adult Christians must see the difference between Christianity and their own culture. They need to be as honest about themselves as the kids are. They must care about one another in the way that God intended. (A biblical description of the early Christians came from the people around them: "See how they love one another.") Adults must recognize that some radical changes are needed in the church. And they must rely on the teachings of Scripture as basic to the faith.

Firm, even dogmatic, biblical teachings do not offend the Jesus kids. "Tell it straight," they say. Their communal leaders are very dogmatic about scriptural truth. But the dogma must be biblical, not cultural. The Jesus kids know very well that some of the churches that pride themselves in being "Bible centered" are not Bible centered at all. They preach about a saved soul and ignore the real business of belonging to, and following, Jesus Christ. The Jesus kids want the teachings of the Bible, not the teachings of an institution that is more influenced by the cultural and social drives of its members than it is by the discipleship and Christian life-style taught in the Bible.

All must grow in the Christian faith together. Every church member, young and old, must approach the teachings of God anew, committed and ready to do whatever God is saying. Each attitude and custom should be reevaluated in the light of Scripture, and people must be able to teach one another the meaning of true discipleship. Love needs to become the binding force of the Christian family, so that persons seek one another's guidance and admit honestly when help is needed to follow Jesus.

New life in the church is not consistent with the rigid maintenance of a particular form of church worship and organization. If "an order of worship" stifles worship, it should be put aside. If people have become spectators, the clergyman should become the teacher of the serving church, not the one who "runs the church." The churches must allow people to meet where they want to, even if in a home or storefront. The church is the body of Christ, not an organization that tries to see how many people it can get into the same room on Sunday morning. The small "family group" of the commune is building some real Christians.

The church will have to accept the risk of people going off occasionally on some theological tangent. If the family of God is receptive and responsive, correct teaching will be sought. When they have no place to go for teaching, people tend to go off the track theologically. People who love one another and pray for one another and are available to one another as teachers and counselors usually grow stronger than the spectator Christian who is "told" what to believe. The spectator Christian, with no biblical basis to guide him when he is confronted by false doctrine, is the one who leaves the faith. The free, creative, biblically centered people of God will grow and will be attractive to the Jesus kids. The warmth of their Christian love will draw people and hold them as they mature in the faith.

"For too long," a pastor said, "we've been talking about giving the kids popcorn and Kool-Aid, when they've been debating between acid and grass."

The kids don't want church programs given to them. They want a family of God, growing together and helping one another. The pastor explained that kids who have sniffed glue in the seventh grade and played with sex in the eighth do not want artificial church meetings or youth fellowship discussions about "Should Christians go to dances?" They want depth; they want content. They want to find the Christ who can meet them in the midst of a very rough world. They know what temptation is. They know how rough life can be. When they worship, it must be out of life, not a role they act out between the prelude and postlude on Sunday morning.

The Reverend Father Dale Melczek, associate pastor of St. Sylvester Roman Catholic Church in Warren, Michigan, knows where it's at with the kids. He said in a *Detroit Free Press* interview that he was glad that the Jesus kids meet in his church. Some five hundred young people gather in the church on Friday evenings. He is pleased because the youth "come to know the Lord Jesus better and to appreciate the Bible. The big thing is the kids don't go on a bummer, but accept Jesus."

An adult, active in the Jesus movement, commented that he was excited about the outpouring of God's power in the young people but disturbed by the lack of people, mature in the faith, who could teach these new Christians. They are struggling alone or in groups, often being taught by people who know little more than they do.

The kids who make it to a Christian commune seem to grow best. There, people care for one another and teach each other. The kids do not have to be on their own, and that is important. Having come out of a questioning, doubting, sometimes drug-filled world, they need teachers who understand what they think and feel and can teach them biblical content out of the realities of life. But there are more young Christians than there are communes and teachers.

A Jesus kid, mature in the faith for his short six months as a believer, said: "If the churches would get going, it would be a tremendous help to the Jesus people."

Even though he prefers a pentecostal charismatic church, he wished that all of the churches would show some enthusiasm for Jesus so that the kids would see that they had many churches to go to for teaching.

"It hurts their chances for spiritual growth when they see cool, unenthusiastic people in the churches. Able or not, those churches will not be given the opportunity to teach the kids, and the kids will have that many fewer teachers."

The short supply of teachers has sent many Jesus kids back to teachers who really do not have much to offer, but at least give the impression that they personally know and love the Lord. One Bible study leader teaches only "the seven gifts of the Spirit." When he has completed the seventh study, he starts all over again. That is all his young people get!

If the church people who have been dragging along in the Christian faith would pray to be renewed, then the kids on the streets would realize that they, too, love the Lord and they would go to them for teaching. Alert leaders of the Jesus kids are begging the church to "wake up, follow Christ, get with the Spirit or be left behind."

Richard Hogue, a twenty-four-year-old evangelist, told a Southern Baptist reporter, "If we don't disciple these kids — if this Jesus movement folds, it will be the churches' responsibility.

If we just bend a little, I think we'll see the greatest revival there has even been. But if this Jesus movement don't go, man, you can just put it down: the church blew it."

A sinful past, or experiences similar to those of the Jesus kids, is not necessary to have a spirit of enthusiasm for Jesus. People who cannot point to a great contrast in their lives brought about by a dramatic conversion can still be excited about their Christian life.

The director of a Christian center logically reasons: "Was Jesus an ex-drug addict, or an ex-taxgatherer, or an ex-anything? Then how did he manage to relate so well to such people? How did he win a hearing? He was able because he came to people. It is ridiculous to think that God can use people better if they have an extensive history of sin. The Holy Spirit has never sinned. He does the work of God. To have a past history of drug addiction, or of anything, has nothing to do with spiritual knowledge, ability, or intelligence. We don't need an impressive testimony. We need to be renewed again by the Spirit of God."

The Jesus kids have a message to give to the church. There is a new spirit moving in the streets. It is a spirit that declining and closing churches seem to have lost. The present time is crucial for the church.

Around the country as the Jesus movement spreads, many churches in many different denominations are coming alive. The question that the Jesus kids are asking is: "Will the churches come alive in time?"

The revival in the streets can still spill over into the church, and church people can once again be the responsive people of God, biblically orthodox in both doctrine and life-style. The spirit of new life in Christ can permeate everywhere.

The Jesus kids would welcome a response from the church; they cannot grow and serve the Lord on their own. They are disjointed, wanting to get out the message of Jesus and eager to grow in the faith, yet they are too unstructured for the long haul — the mission that will continue after they are grown. They need the church.

The church can protect the young Christians from people who would capture them for their own ego-building programs.

The church has the resources and maturity to add theological and intellectual depth to a movement that needs roots.

94

The church can offer the sense of history, the continuity of the Christian faith through the ages that the "now" generation has missed.

And, if it will bend a little, the church can teach the great concepts of worship and the powerful holiness of God that the casual young need to know.

In self-giving love, the people of the church can be the mothers and fathers in Christ that the love-starved young Christians want and need.

But the need is not all one-sided. The church needs the Jesus kids, too. Many Christians are looking at the Jesus kids and starting to recall that there was a time when the church of Jesus Christ was vibrant and alive and had a commitment to him that was greater than anything else.

The church is shaking itself and rising. The enthusiasm of the Jesus kids is beginning to revive the church. Too long there has been a tendency to be overly sophisticated, even blasé about the redemptive, wonder-filled power of God. Too long the great joy and deep pleasure of knowing the person and the work of God's Son has been played down.

The Jesus kids can check the cool, unresponsive ways that many church people have had toward one another and toward God. The Jesus kids won't let the dust continue to gather — the church needs these kids!

The church always has had problems, but also it always has had the ability to change. It never has been deaf to the promptings of the Holy Spirit; it is not deaf now. Therein is its strength.

The young are neither mature enough nor experienced enough to cope with the problems they face; the church is. If the Jesus kids see a church that is alive, that is dedicated to serving Christ, and that is working at its problems, they will be attracted to it. As the longing to belong again in a personal way to Jesus Christ stirs the church, the kids will see a new spirit, respond to it, and generate more of it.

God is using two generations of his people to build one another so that he can form a body of believers mighty in its strengths, humble in its weaknesses, healing and redemptive in its ministry.

The Spirit of God is moving in the land. He is not selective.

Whether the people be Jesus kids, Jesus freaks, Methodists, Baptists, or Roman Catholics, "We, though many, are one body in Christ, and individually members one of another . . ." (Romans 12:5, RSV). This is the way God has always wanted his church to be. It can be that way now.

When the revival in the streets joins the revival in the church, men and women everywhere will once again hear and believe the words:

"He lives!"

THE JESUS KiDS

Here is a report on a youth
movement that has startled
adults across the nation. Salvation and baptism in the name
of Jesus have replaced drugs
and demonstrations in the
lives of thousands of young
people. These young people
claim to have found a new out-
look on life through faith in
Jesus and an almost literal interpretation of the Bible. Many
adults have wondered if these
claims are really true and
whether this attachment to
Jesus will really last. The author traveled across the country to talk to the Jesus Kids,
their parents, pastors, and
other adults, including policemen; and here he tells what he
discovered about the Jesus
movement.

Roger C. Palms is a campus
chaplain at Michigan State University. A graduate of Wayne
State University, Michigan State
University, and of Eastern Baptist Theological Seminary, he
served as a pastor before as-
suming his present responsibility. He has also written arti-
cles for a number of magazines
and newspapers.

Cover Design by Janie Russell